A hot ticket to English success from CGP

There are a lot of English skills to conquer in Year 2, and the best way of getting to grips with them is practice, practice, practice. Luckily, this CGP book covers just that.

Containing a heap of skills from the Year 2 curriculum, it's got fun activities, comprehension texts and examples. There's something for every day of summer term. Blimey!

We've also upped the fun-factor even more with bright and colourful pictures. Wherever you are — in class, at home, on a horse — it's daily practice for anywhere!

What CGP is all about

Our sole aim here at CGP is to produce the highest quality books
— carefully written, immaculately presented and
dangerously close to being funny.

Then we work our socks off to get them out to you
— at the cheapest possible prices.

Contents

☑ Use the tick boxes to help keep a record of which tests have been attempted.

Published by CGP

ISBN: 978 1 78908 680 5

Editors: Izzy Bowen, Eleanor Claringbold, Rachel Craig-McFeely, Rebecca Greaves, Rebecca Russell, Sean Walsh
With thanks to Juliette Green and Holly Robinson for the proofreading.
With thanks to Lottie Edwards for the copyright research.

Cover and Graphics used throughout the book © www.edu-clips.com

Printed by Elanders Ltd, Newcastle upon Tyne.
Based on the classic CGP style created by Richard Parsons.

How to Use this Book

- This book contains <u>60 pages of daily English practice</u>.

- We've split them into <u>12 sections</u> — that's roughly one for <u>each week</u> of the Year 2 <u>Summer term</u>.

- Each week is made up of <u>5 pages</u>, so there's one for <u>every school day</u> of the term (Monday – Friday).

- Each page should take about <u>10 minutes</u> to complete.

- The pages contain a <u>mix</u> of topics from <u>Year 2</u> English. <u>New Year 2 topics</u> are gradually introduced as you go through the book.

- The pages <u>increase in difficulty</u> as you progress through the book.

- <u>Answers</u> can be found at the <u>back</u> of the book.

- Each page looks something like this:

The <u>Week</u> and the <u>Day</u> are shown at the top of the page.

The <u>instruction</u> the pupil needs to follow is in the box at the top of the page.

There's an <u>example</u> at the top of the page. The <u>correct</u> answer is shown in red. <u>Talk</u> the pupil through the <u>instruction</u> and the <u>example</u> so they know what to do.

There's a <u>score box</u> at the <u>bottom</u> of the page. Use this to <u>keep track</u> of how well the pupil has done.

There is a range of <u>questions</u> for the pupil to <u>answer</u>.

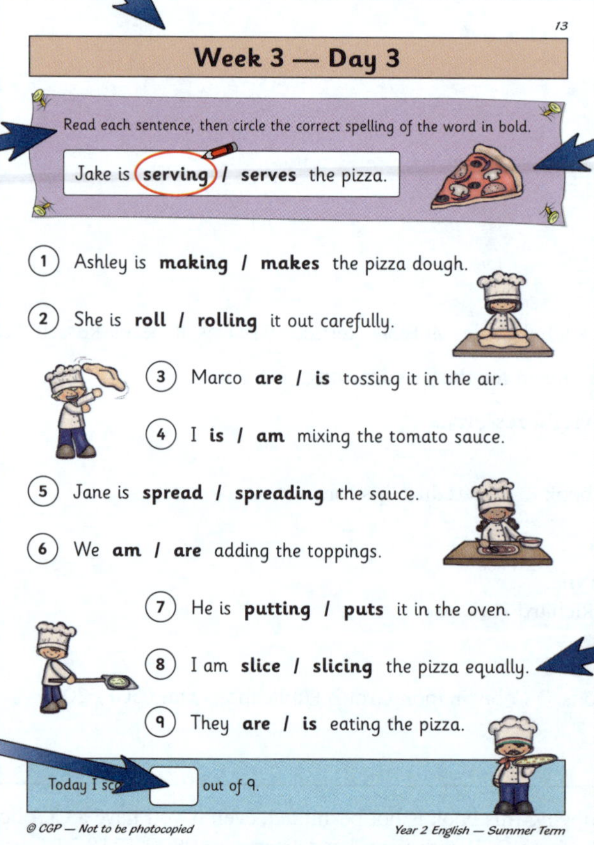

Week 1 — Day 1

Read each sentence, then circle the
correct spelling of the word in bold.

There was **nuthing** / **nothing** in the chest.

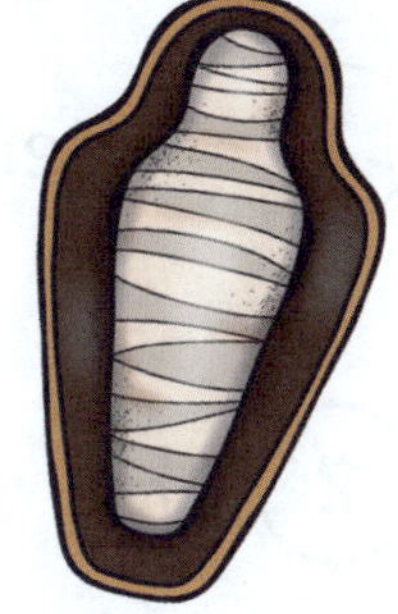

(1) The **treasure** / **treashure** was in the pyramid.

(2) The **uther** / **other** mummy was much scarier.

(3) I waved my hand to **swot** / **swat** away the fly.

(4) A **swarm** / **sworm** of insects ate the crops.

(5) We set off on the long **journey** / **journee**.

(6) The queen **wolked** / **walked** by the river.

(7) They **werked** / **worked** hard on the statue.

(8) I couldn't see in the **darkness** / **darkeness** of the tomb.

(9) I was full of **excitment** / **excitement** to visit Egypt.

Today I scored [ ] out of 9.

Year 2 English — Summer Term

Week 1 — Day 2

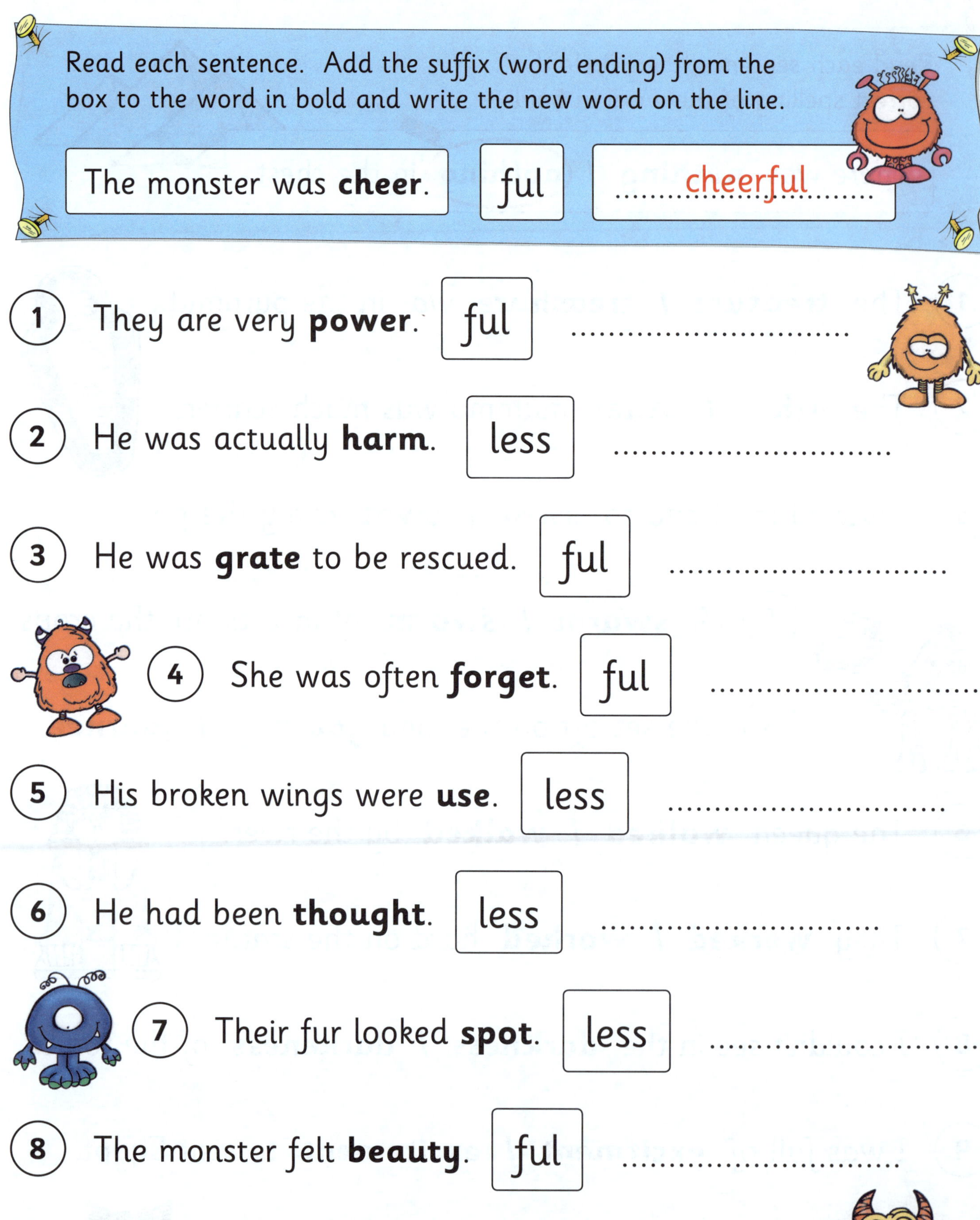

Read each sentence. Add the suffix (word ending) from the box to the word in bold and write the new word on the line.

The monster was **cheer**. | ful | .... cheerful ....

1. They are very **power**. | ful | ....

2. He was actually **harm**. | less | ....

3. He was **grate** to be rescued. | ful | ....

4. She was often **forget**. | ful | ....

5. His broken wings were **use**. | less | ....

6. He had been **thought**. | less | ....

7. Their fur looked **spot**. | less | ....

8. The monster felt **beauty**. | ful | ....

Today I scored ☐ out of 8.

Week 1 — Day 3

Circle the correct word to complete each sentence.

 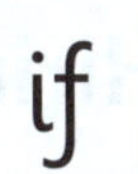

She chose the coat (**because**) **if** she liked purple.

1. Nan promised us some crumbs **that** **if** we behaved.

2. Mia hid in the nest **because** **that** she was scared.

3. We ran away **when** **that** the humans were near.

4. Leo's whiskers twitch **when** **that** he's confused.

5. His ears pricked up **if** **that** he was angry.

6. I like any dish **because** **that** has cheese in it.

7. Em had grey fur **that** **when** was just like her dad's.

8. Lou gave a squeak **that** **because** she was excited.

Today I scored [ ] out of 8.

Year 2 English — Summer Term

Week 1 — Day 4

Read the text, then answer the questions.

Now Hiring Chocolate Tasters!

We are looking for three people to join our team of chocolate tasters at Bea's Chocolate Factory. The ideal people for the job will know exactly what makes a good chocolate. To apply, all you have to do is fill in a simple form. The lucky three people will be invited to join our yearly chocolate fountain party and our baking competition. If you love chocolate and sweet treats, this is the job for you!

1 How many people are the chocolate factory looking for?

....

2 Which of these words is the closest in meaning to '**ideal**'?

worst ☐   hungry ☐   perfect ☐   happy ☐

3 How do you apply for the job?

....

4 Write down one event you get invited to if you get the job. 

....

Today I scored ☐ out of 4.

Week 1 — Day 5

Read the poem, then answer the questions.

Stargazing

Lying on the soft, green grass,
Pia looked up at the stars one night.
The smaller ones glittered like gems,
The bigger ones shone and were bright.
Every so often, as if by magic,
A shooting star caught Pia's eye.
It left behind a long trail of gold,
Carving a path through the deep blue sky.

1 How does the narrator describe the bigger stars?

dull ☐   glittering ☐   bright ☐   pretty ☐

2 Add either 'if' or 'when' to complete this sentence.

Pia was lying down .... she saw a shooting star.

3 What colour was the shooting star's trail?

....

4 Write the correct suffix (word ending) for the word in bold.

Pia thought the stars were **wonder**...............

Today I scored ☐ out of 4.

Year 2 English — Summer Term

Week 2 — Day 1

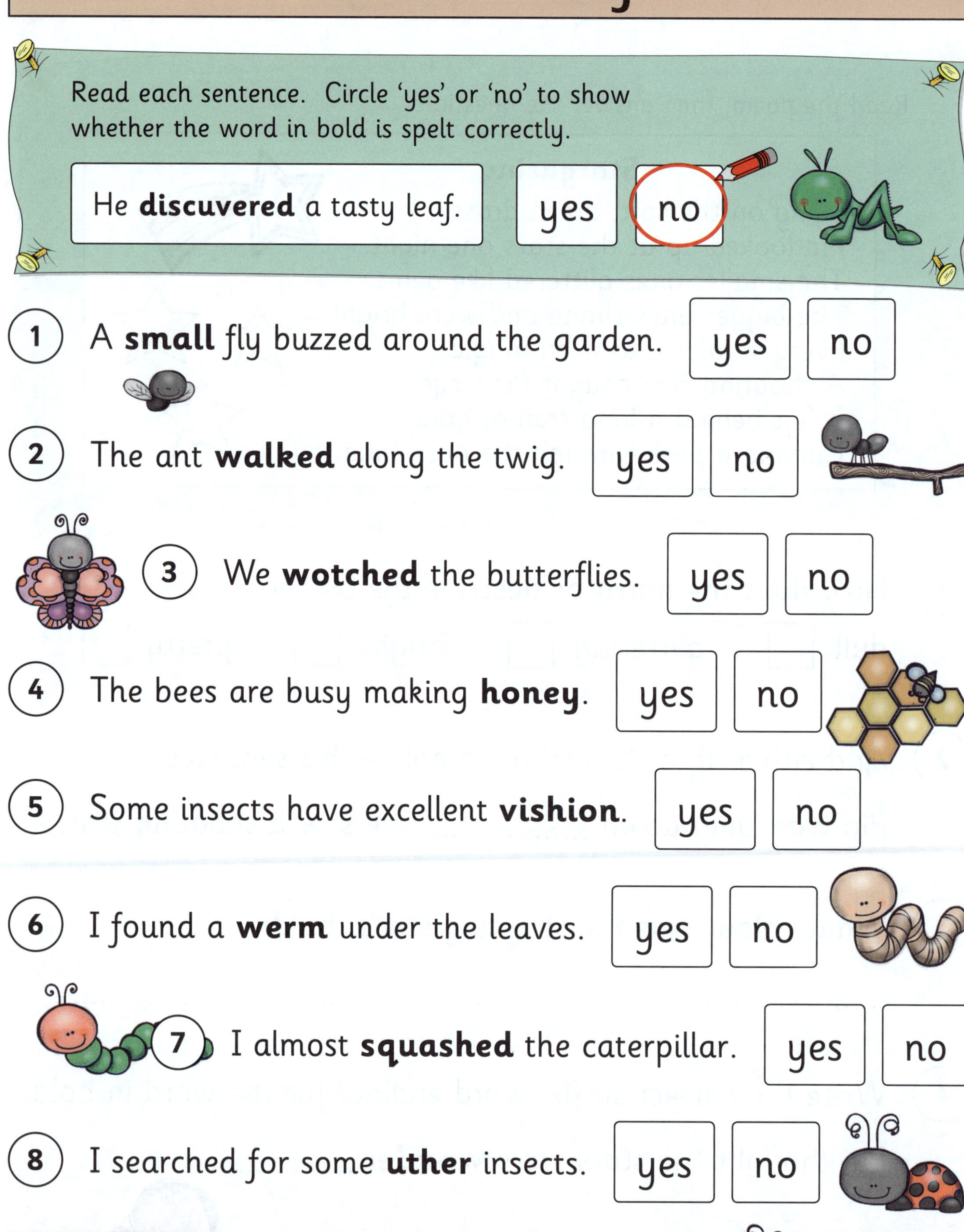

Read each sentence. Circle 'yes' or 'no' to show whether the word in bold is spelt correctly.

He **discuvered** a tasty leaf.   yes   no

1. A **small** fly buzzed around the garden.   yes   no

2. The ant **walked** along the twig.   yes   no

3. We **wotched** the butterflies.   yes   no

4. The bees are busy making **honey**.   yes   no

5. Some insects have excellent **vishion**.   yes   no

6. I found a **werm** under the leaves.   yes   no

7. I almost **squashed** the caterpillar.   yes   no

8. I searched for some **uther** insects.   yes   no

Today I scored ☐ out of 8.

Week 2 — Day 2

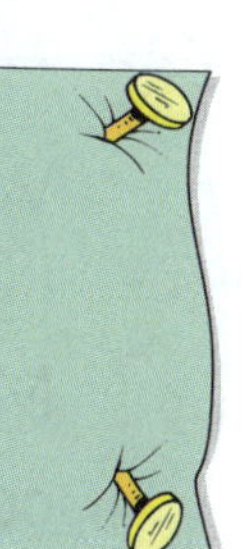

A group of children are playing a game where some of them pretend to be teachers and some of them pretend to be pupils. Read what they have to say below and then answer the questions.

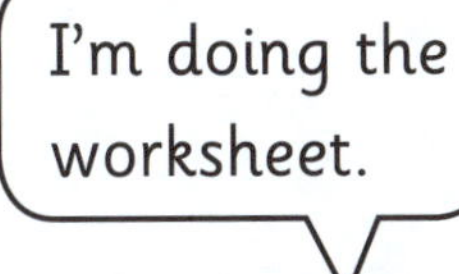

Liz

Abe

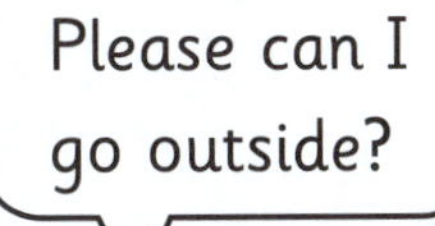

Ruby

Ben

1 Who asks a question? ....

2 Who gives a command? ....

3 Who makes a statement? ....

4 Who makes an exclamation? ....

5 Which two children are pretending to be teachers?

.... and ....

Today I scored ☐ out of 6.

Year 2 English — Summer Term

Week 2 — Day 3

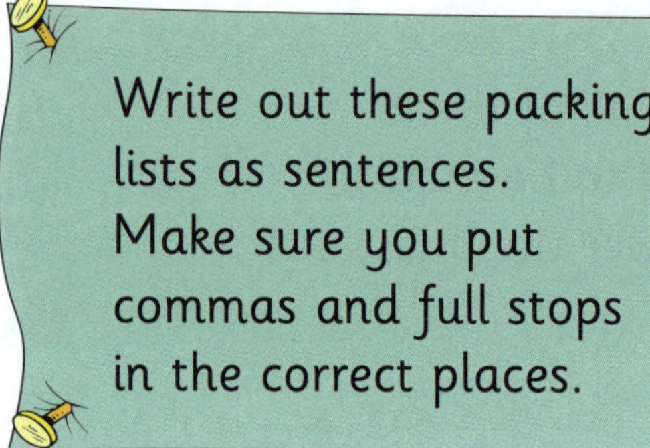

Write out these packing lists as sentences. Make sure you put commas and full stops in the correct places.

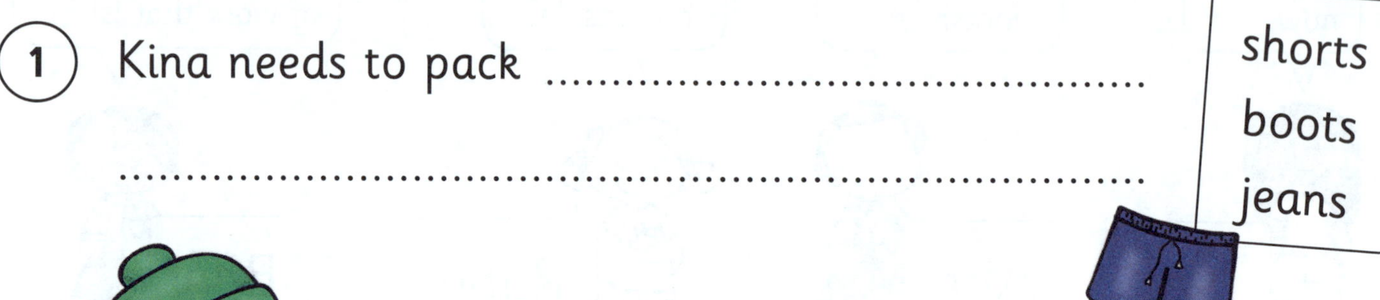

1 Kina needs to pack ....

....

2 Jason needs to pack ....

....

3 Lewis needs to pack ....

....

4 Tess needs to pack ....

....

Today I scored [　] out of 4.

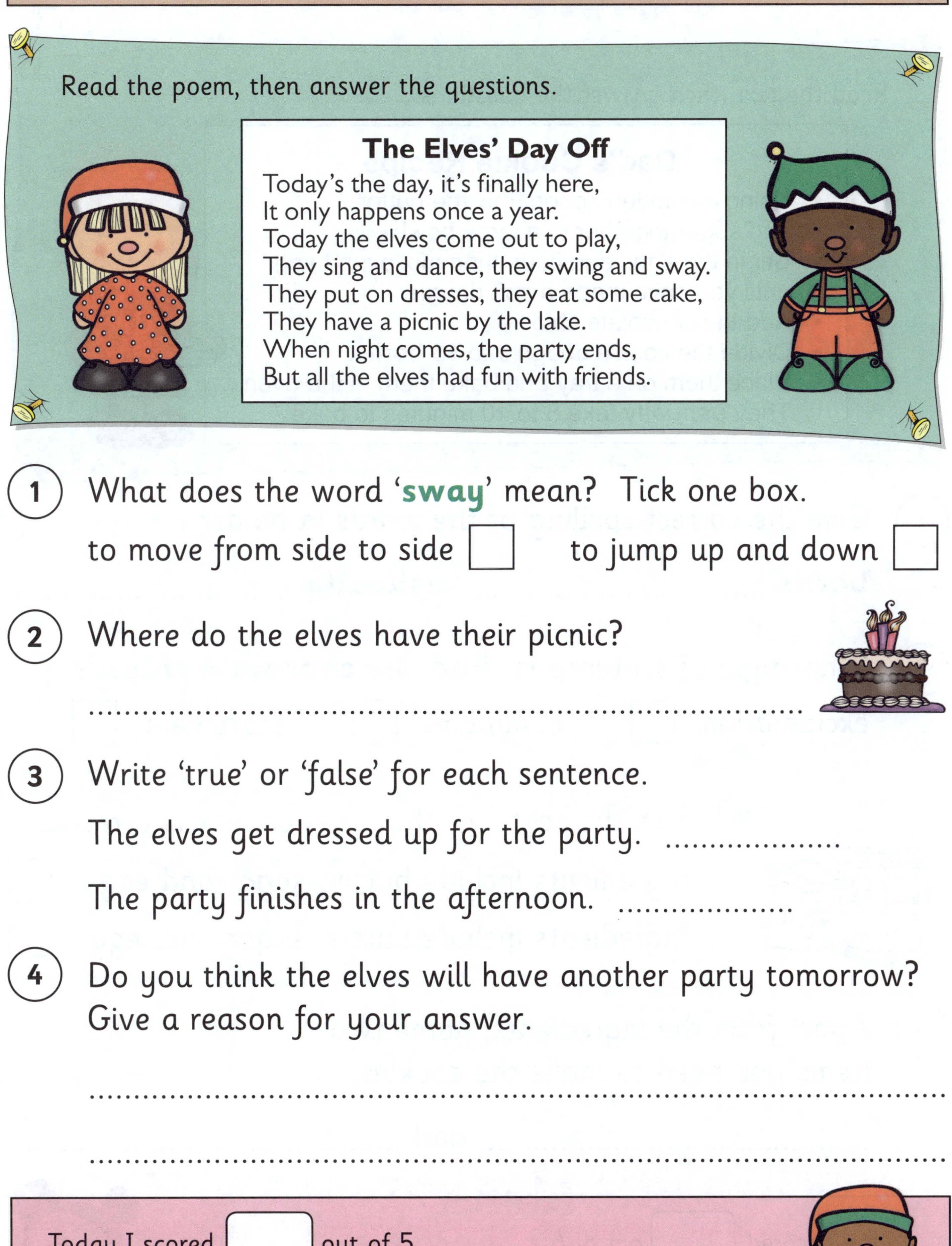

Week 2 — Day 4

Read the poem, then answer the questions.

The Elves' Day Off

Today's the day, it's finally here,
It only happens once a year.
Today the elves come out to play,
They sing and dance, they swing and sway.
They put on dresses, they eat some cake,
They have a picnic by the lake.
When night comes, the party ends,
But all the elves had fun with friends.

1 What does the word 'sway' mean? Tick one box.

to move from side to side ☐   to jump up and down ☐

2 Where do the elves have their picnic?

....

3 Write 'true' or 'false' for each sentence.

The elves get dressed up for the party. ....

The party finishes in the afternoon. ....

4 Do you think the elves will have another party tomorrow?
Give a reason for your answer.

....

....

Today I scored ☐ out of 5.

    Year 2 English — Summer Term

Week 2 — Day 5

Read the text, then answer the questions.

Dad's Cookie Recipe

- Using a wooden spoon, mix the butter and sugar together in a large bowl.
- Stir in the eggs and flour, then mix everything until you have made a soft dough.
- Add the chocolate chips.
- Divide the cookie dough into 15 **borlls**.
- Place them on a tray and bake them in the oven. They **ushually** take 8 to 10 minutes to bake.

1) Give the correct spelling of the words in bold.

borlls .... **ushually** ....

2) What type of sentence is '**Add the chocolate chips.**'?

exclamation ☐   command ☐   statement ☐

3) Tick the sentence that uses commas correctly.

Ingredients include butter, sugar and eggs. ☐

Ingredients include butter, sugar and, eggs. ☐

4) Apart from the ingredients, name two items you need to make the cookies.

.... and ....

Today I scored ☐ out of 6.

Week 3 — Day 1

The words in bold below are spelt incorrectly.
Write the correct spellings on the lines.

I hope I don't **forl**. .... *fall* ....

1. Tara is an ice **hockie** player. ....

2. Anton is the **werld** champion. ....

3. I watched the contest on **televission**. ....

4. They waited for the judge's **decizion**. ....

5. My **bruther** came third. ....

6. He wears **wharm** clothes. ....

7. Leah was **aworded** a medal. ....

8. We watched the skater in **amazment**. ....

Today I scored [ ] out of 8.

Week 3 — Day 2

For each sentence below, add a **question mark**, **exclamation mark** and **full stop** to the gaps. Then circle the letter that should be a **capital letter**.

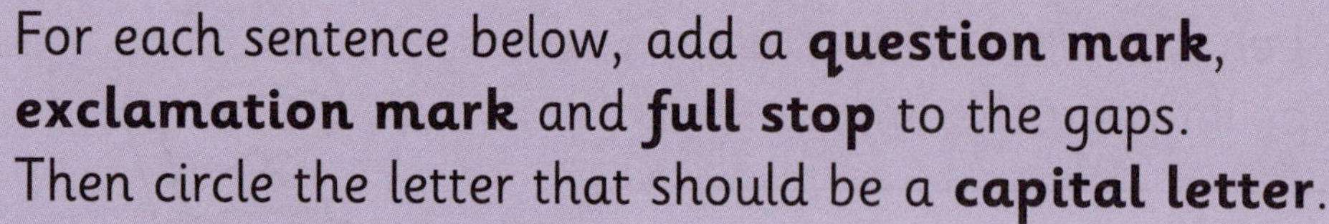

I've got a new game........ Have you played it before?...... Oh no, we're missing a piece!......

1. "Can you shuffle the cards, Beth........" I asked. Beth gave me ten cards........ "don't look at what cards I have......." I shouted.

2. Let's make a tower........ what colour blocks should we use........ How beautiful it looks........

3. "What a great game chess is........" Cam said excitedly. "we play it every Sunday........ Do you want to go first........"

4. shall we play hide and seek........ I'll count to twenty........ Hooray, I've found you........

Today I scored ☐ out of 16.

Week 3 — Day 3

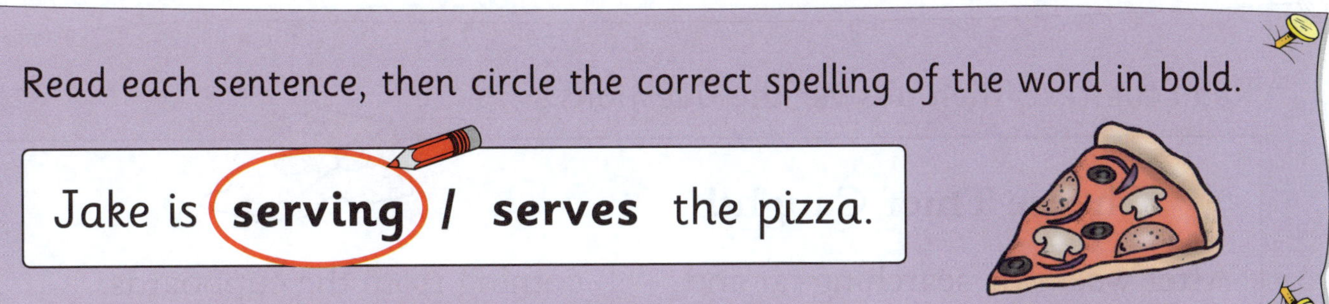

Read each sentence, then circle the correct spelling of the word in bold.

Jake is **serving** / **serves** the pizza.

1 Ashley is **making** / **makes** the pizza dough.

2 She is **roll** / **rolling** it out carefully.

3 Marco **are** / **is** tossing it in the air.

4 I **is** / **am** mixing the tomato sauce.

5 Jane is **spread** / **spreading** the sauce.

6 We **am** / **are** adding the toppings.

7 He is **putting** / **puts** it in the oven.

8 I am **slice** / **slicing** the pizza equally.

9 They **are** / **is** eating the pizza.

Today I scored [ ] out of 9.

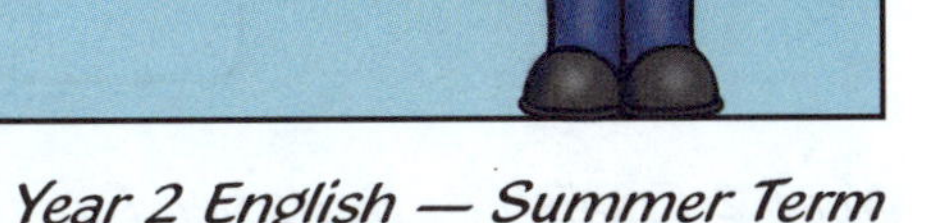

Year 2 English — Summer Term

Week 3 — Day 4

Read the text, then answer the questions.

Cheese Thief Caught!

After weeks of searching far and wide, a cheese thief has been caught. The culprit, a rat called Robin D. Bree, was found nibbling on some cheese and crackers in the cupboard of a café last Sunday. The café owner called the police after she heard a strange noise coming from the cupboards. Once caught, Robin also confessed to robbing the cheese factory last week and to stealing a large cheesecake from the bakery the week before. He said that he couldn't return the cheese even if he wanted to.

1) Write 'true' or 'false' for each sentence.

The café is the first place Robin stole from. ....

Robin was found in a cupboard. ....

2) What did Robin steal from the bakery?

....

3) What do you think '**confessed**' might mean?

owned up ☐   lied ☐   stole ☐

4) What do you think happened to the stolen cheese?

....

Today I scored ☐ out of 5.

Week 3 — Day 5

Read the text, then answer the questions.

Catch of the Day

Sam sat in the boat with a big frown on his face. He didn't get any **pleashure** from fishing.

"Can we go home now?" he asked his mum. "I'm bored."

"Not until you've caught something," she said, handing him back his fishing rod. Sam took it with a scowl and sat waiting for a fish. At last, he felt something tug at the fishing line. Suddenly excited to catch something, he reeled it in, but it wasn't a fish that appeared from the **worter**. It was a big, orange, slimy monster!

1 Give the correct spelling of the words in bold.

pleashure .... **worter** ....

2 Tick the sentence that uses the present tense correctly.

Sam is sits in the little boat. ☐

Sam is sitting in the little boat. ☐

3 Why do you think Sam's mum hands him the fishing rod?

....

4 How do Sam's feelings about fishing change?

He becomes more excited about it. ☐

He becomes less excited about it. ☐

Today I scored ☐ out of 5.

Week 4 — Day 1

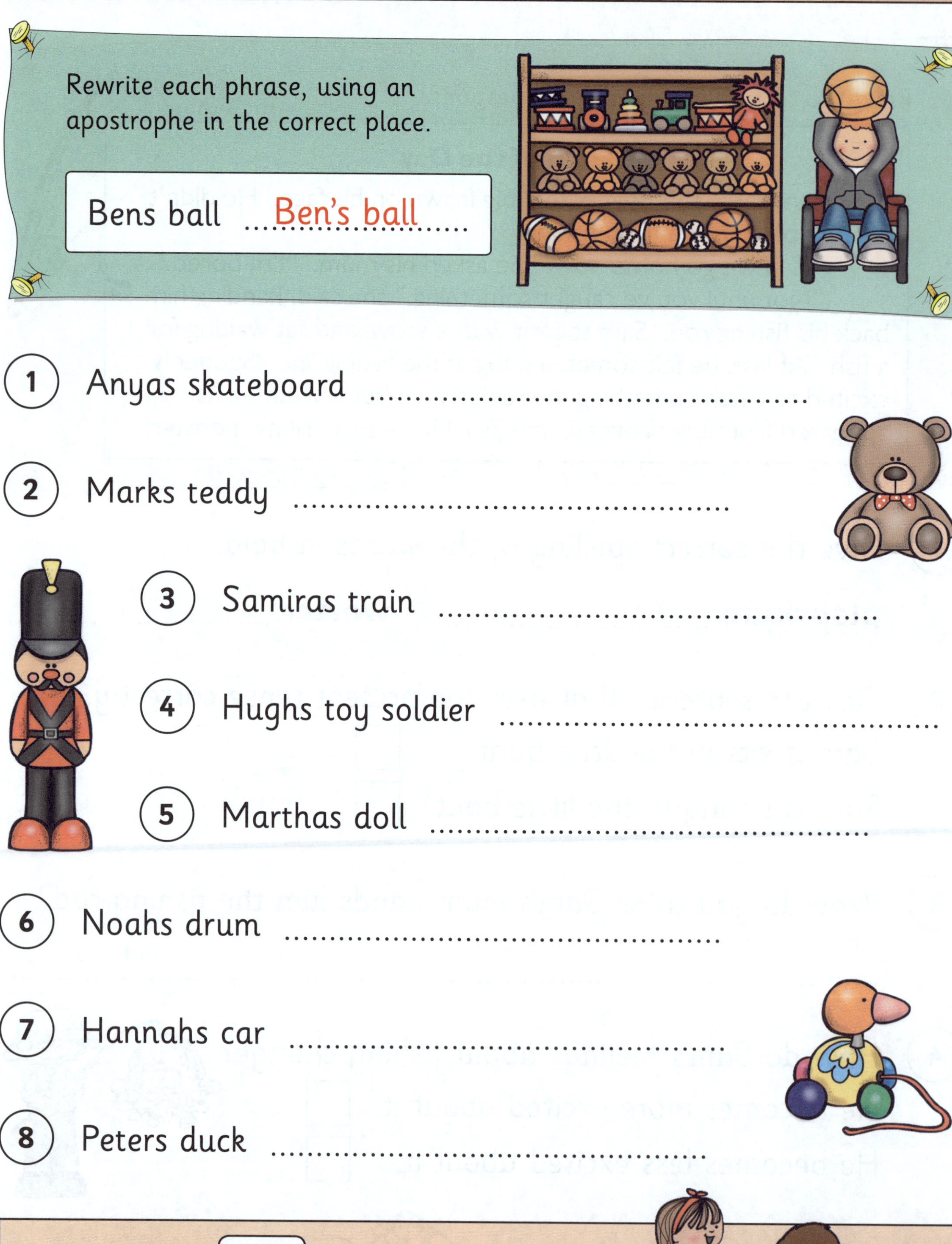

Rewrite each phrase, using an apostrophe in the correct place.

Bens ball .....Ben's ball.....

1. Anyas skateboard ....

2. Marks teddy ....

3. Samiras train ....

4. Hughs toy soldier ....

5. Marthas doll ....

6. Noahs drum ....

7. Hannahs car ....

8. Peters duck ....

Today I scored ☐ out of 8.

Week 4 — Day 2

Write either '**ful**', '**less**' or '**ly**' to complete each word in bold. Then, for each picture at the bottom of the page, write the sentence number it links to.

> Orisa feels happy and **joy**.ful.........

1 Oscar was **fear**............. that a spider would crawl on him.

2 Molly **quiet**............. told her sister a secret.

3 My dog has a loud bark but she's **harm**.............

4 Tim **proud**............. accepted his medal when he won.

5 Jaxon was very **forget**.............

6 Kameela's necklace was **price**............. to her.

Today I scored [ ] out of 11.

Year 2 English — Summer Term

Week 4 — Day 3

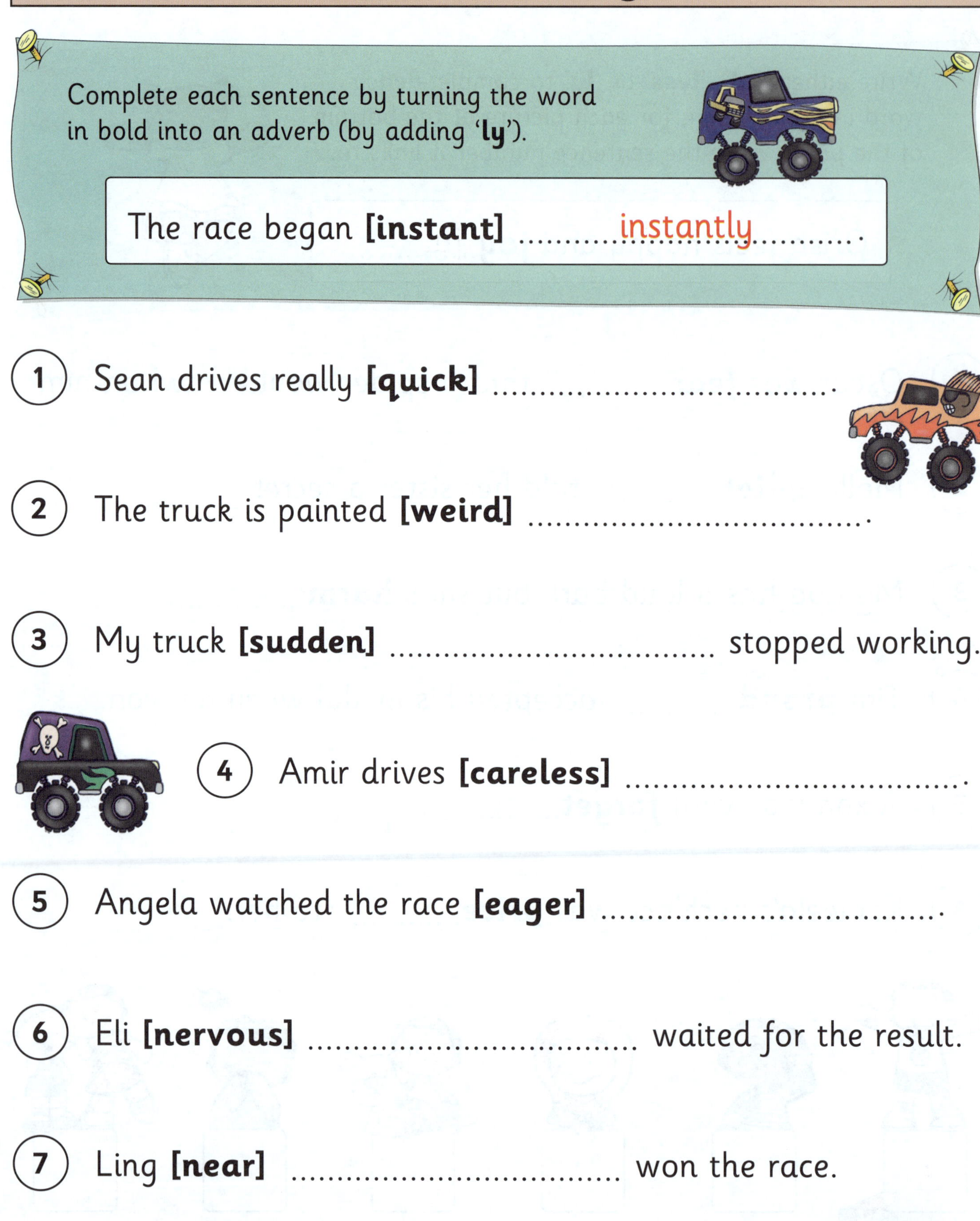

Complete each sentence by turning the word in bold into an adverb (by adding '**ly**').

The race began [**instant**] ....instantly............. .

1. Sean drives really [**quick**] ....

2. The truck is painted [**weird**] ....

3. My truck [**sudden**] .... stopped working.

4. Amir drives [**careless**] ....

5. Angela watched the race [**eager**] ....

6. Eli [**nervous**] .... waited for the result.

7. Ling [**near**] .... won the race.

Today I scored [   ] out of 7.

Week 4 — Day 4

Read the text, then answer the questions.

The Secret Superhero

Ama only had 15 minutes to save the world. This would panic most other people, but not Ama. She had done this many times before. You see, Ama had secret superpowers that not even her parents knew about.

Ama took a deep breath and started planning. She could use her power of invisibility to creep up on the baddie, or she could go up to him and zap him with her laser fingers. Ama put on her mask, ready to save the world.

1 Write down two of Ama's superpowers.

.... and ....

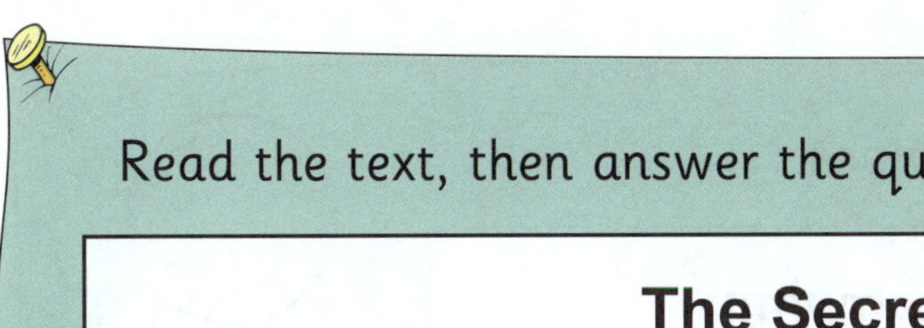

2 Which word means the same as '**creep**'.

sprint ☐   sneak ☐   jump ☐

3 Put a tick next to the sentence that is true.

Ama's parents know about her powers. ☐

Ama wears a superhero mask. ☐

4 Why do you think Ama doesn't panic when she only has 15 minutes to save the world?

....

....

Today I scored ☐ out of 5.

Year 2 English — Summer Term

Week 4 — Day 5

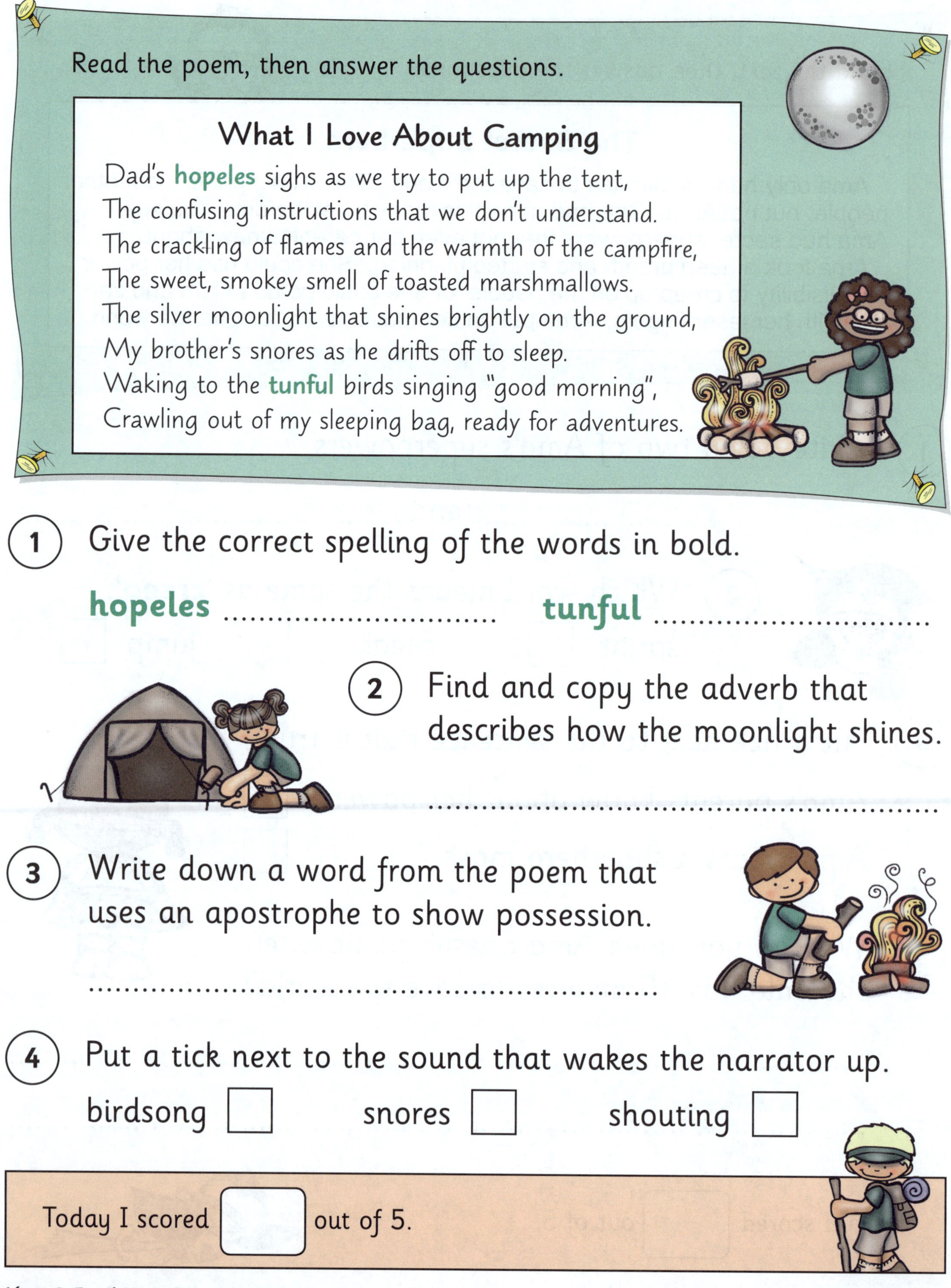

Read the poem, then answer the questions.

What I Love About Camping

Dad's **hopeles** sighs as we try to put up the tent,
The confusing instructions that we don't understand.
The crackling of flames and the warmth of the campfire,
The sweet, smokey smell of toasted marshmallows.
The silver moonlight that shines brightly on the ground,
My brother's snores as he drifts off to sleep.
Waking to the **tunful** birds singing "good morning",
Crawling out of my sleeping bag, ready for adventures.

1 Give the correct spelling of the words in bold.

hopeles .... **tunful** ....

2 Find and copy the adverb that describes how the moonlight shines.

....

3 Write down a word from the poem that uses an apostrophe to show possession.

....

4 Put a tick next to the sound that wakes the narrator up.

birdsong ☐　　snores ☐　　shouting ☐

Today I scored ☐ out of 5.

Week 5 — Day 1

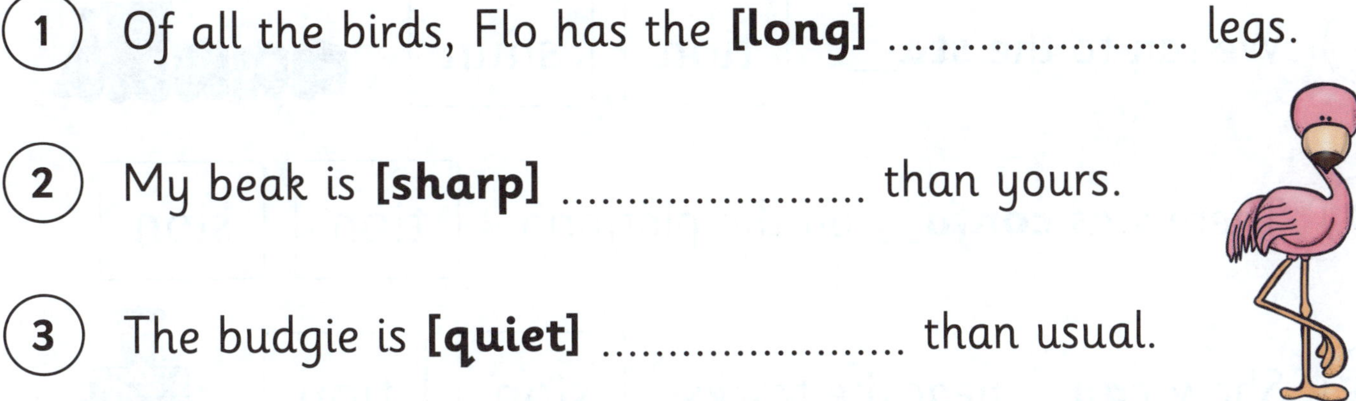

Complete the sentences by adding either 'er' or 'est' to the words in bold.

Rita's feathers are **[bright]** ...brighter... than mine.

1. Of all the birds, Flo has the **[long]** .... legs.

2. My beak is **[sharp]** .... than yours.

3. The budgie is **[quiet]** .... than usual.

4. Pippin is the **[proud]** .... bird of us all.

5. The toucan is **[big]** .... than me.

6. Hummingbirds are **[small]** .... than parrots.

7. The **[great]** .... bird in the group is the puffin.

8. Penguins are **[friendly]** .... than ostriches.

9. The pelican has the **[odd]** .... beak of all birds.

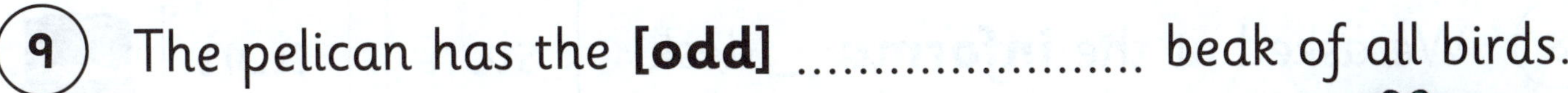

Today I scored ☐ out of 9.

Year 2 English — Summer Term

Week 5 — Day 2

Read each sentence, then circle the letters missing from the word in bold.

The engine is in good **condi__**. | sion | tion

1. We ran to the **sta__**. | tion | shun

2. There was **confu__** on the platform. | tion | sion

3. Show **cau__** near the tracks. | sion | tion

4. The train is in **mo__**. | sion | tion

5. There is a new **ver__** of my toy train. | shun | sion

6. Which **direc__** is the train going in? | sion | tion

7. It was my **deci__** to take the train. | shun | sion

8. We asked at the **informa__** desk. | sion | tion

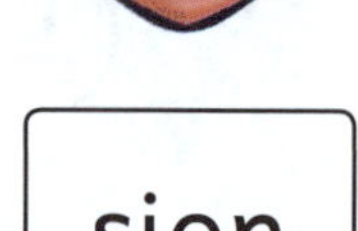

Today I scored [   ] out of 8.

Week 5 — Day 3

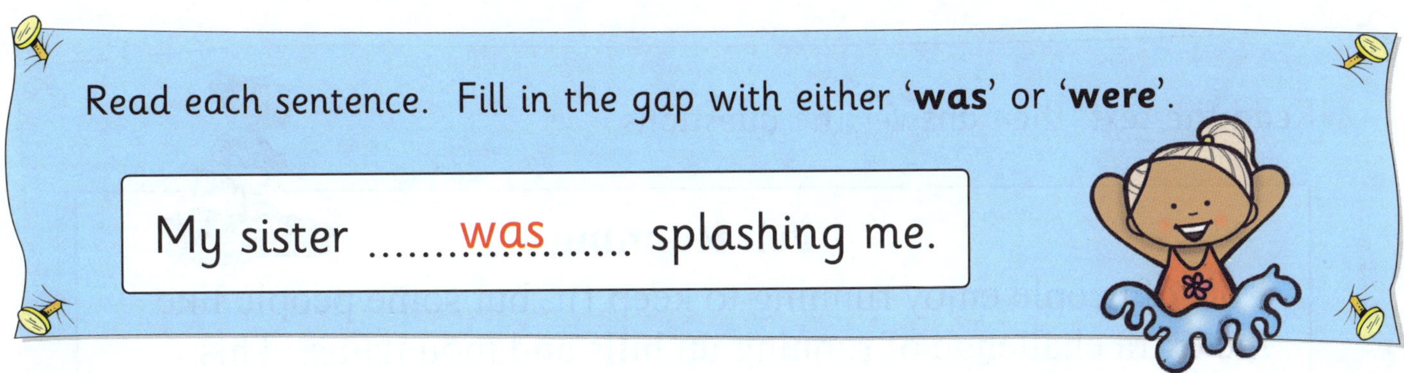

Read each sentence. Fill in the gap with either '**was**' or '**were**'.

My sister ....was........ splashing me.

(1) They .... queuing for the water slide.

(2) Jim .... playing in the fountain.

(3) We .... doing underwater handstands.

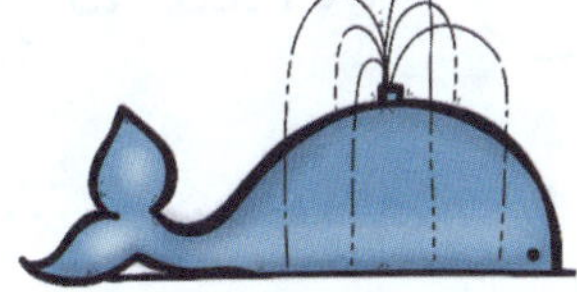

(4) Dad .... watching us from the side.

(5) Chris and Ava .... floating down the lazy river.

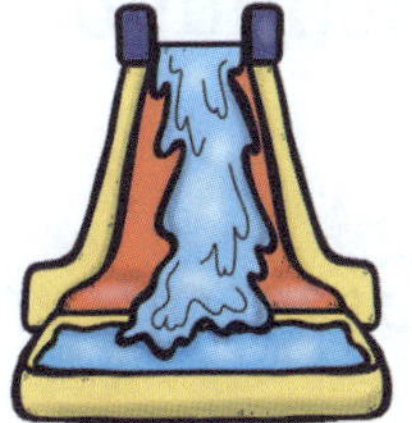

(6) I .... swimming with my friends.

(7) We .... screaming the whole way down the slide.

(8) They .... changing into swimming trunks.

Today I scored [ ] out of 8.

Year 2 English — Summer Term

Week 5 — Day 4

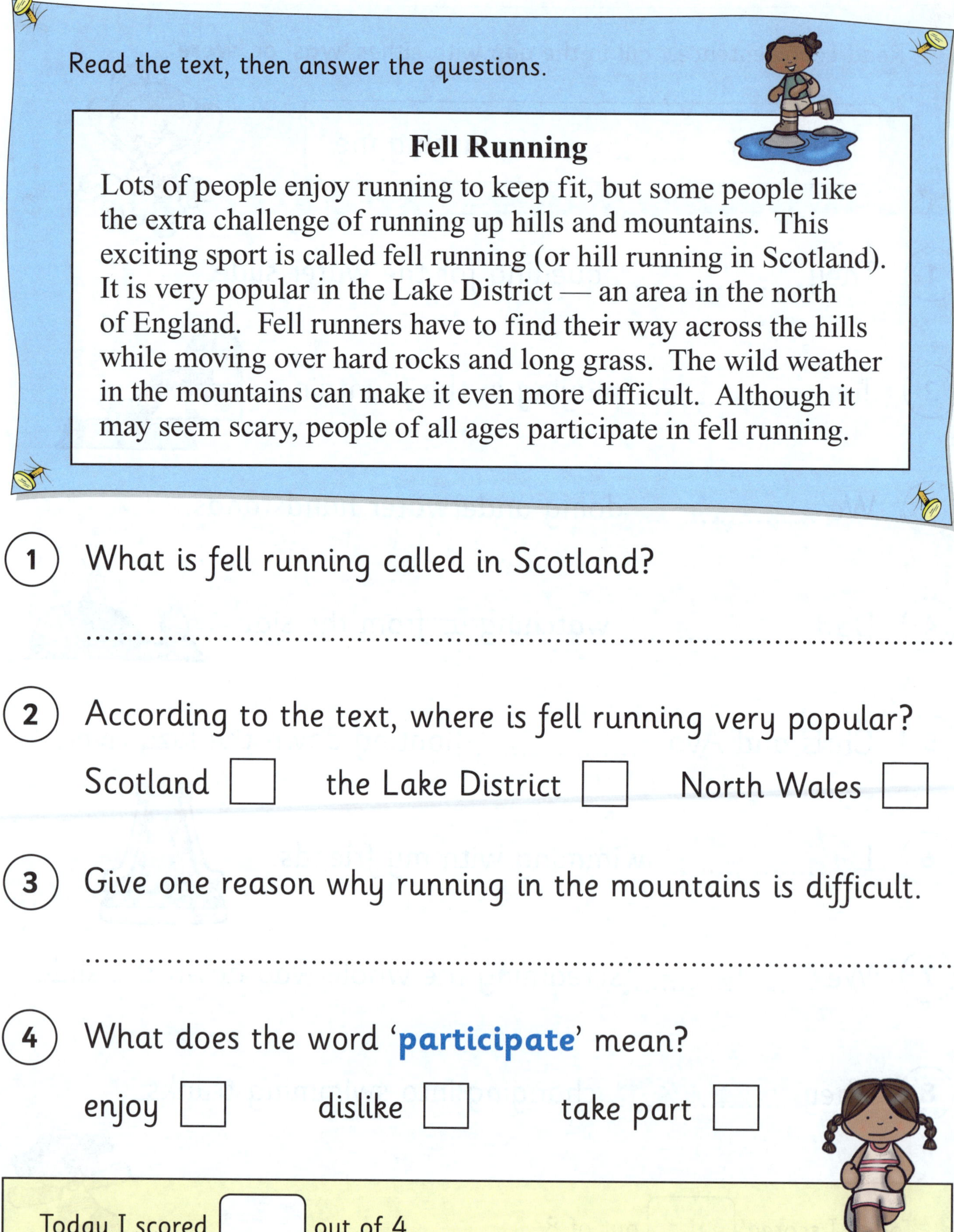

Read the text, then answer the questions.

Fell Running

Lots of people enjoy running to keep fit, but some people like the extra challenge of running up hills and mountains. This exciting sport is called fell running (or hill running in Scotland). It is very popular in the Lake District — an area in the north of England. Fell runners have to find their way across the hills while moving over hard rocks and long grass. The wild weather in the mountains can make it even more difficult. Although it may seem scary, people of all ages participate in fell running.

1) What is fell running called in Scotland?

....

2) According to the text, where is fell running very popular?

Scotland ☐   the Lake District ☐   North Wales ☐

3) Give one reason why running in the mountains is difficult.

....

4) What does the word '**participate**' mean?

enjoy ☐   dislike ☐   take part ☐

Today I scored ☐ out of 4.

Week 5 — Day 5

Read the text, then answer the questions.

The Ruby Mine

Kai turned on his head torch as he journeyed deeper into the mine. He paid close **attension** to where he was putting his feet because the ground was wet and slippery. Out of the corner of his eye, he noticed something sparkle in the light of his torch. He turned to see hundreds of shining rubies stuck into the wall of the mine. He smiled to himself and reached for his shovel. Suddenly, a screeching sound startled him. It was a bat who called the mine home.

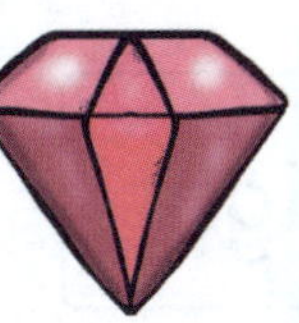

(1) Write the correct spelling of the word in bold.

attension ....

(2) Why do you think Kai turns on his head torch?

....

(3) Give two adjectives that are used to describe the ground in the mine.

.... and ....

(4) Add either 'was' or 'were' to complete this sentence.

Kai .... looking for rubies when he saw the bat.

Today I scored ⬚ out of 5.

   Year 2 English — Summer Term

Week 6 — Day 1

Use the words from the boxes to complete the sentences below. You should only use each word once.

We can .... *see* .... the brave man.

| see | sea |

| night | blue | son | won |

| sun | one | knight | blew |

1. Only .... of them could win.

2. He .... the jousting contest easily.

3. I .... the trumpet when she arrived.

4. The enemy snuck in during the ....

5. He is the .... of the king and queen.

6. She was holding a .... shield.

7. The .... went on a dangerous journey.

8. The .... shone on his armour.

Today I scored [ ] out of 8.

Week 6 — Day 2

Use the words in the boxes to complete the sentences below, adding '**ly**' to turn them into adverbs. Each word should only be used once.

The pig stared ....*hungrily*.......... at the apples. | hungry

| playful | wide | quick | loud | slow | bad |

1 The mud squelched ....

2 The pig dashed around the farmyard ....

3 Mud dripped .... from the pig's face.

4 The pig rolled .... in the mud.

5 The pig smiled .... at the farmer.

6 The farmer told the pig off for behaving ....

Today I scored ☐ out of 6.

Year 2 English — Summer Term

Week 6 — Day 3

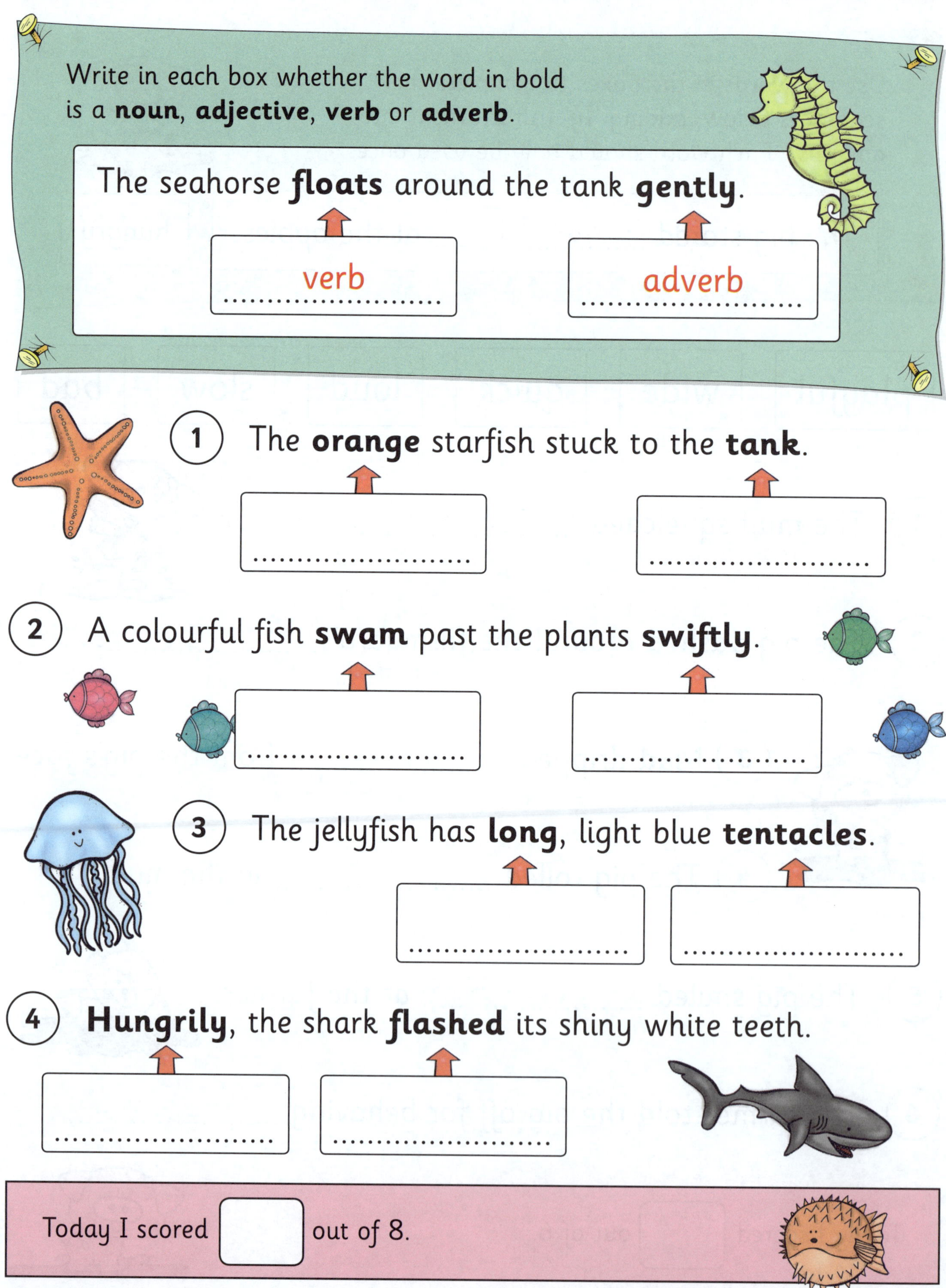

Write in each box whether the word in bold
is a **noun**, **adjective**, **verb** or **adverb**.

The seahorse **floats** around the tank **gently**.

verb

adverb

1 The **orange** starfish stuck to the **tank**.

2 A colourful fish **swam** past the plants **swiftly**.

3 The jellyfish has **long**, light blue **tentacles**.

4 **Hungrily**, the shark **flashed** its shiny white teeth.

Today I scored [ ] out of 8.

Week 6 — Day 4

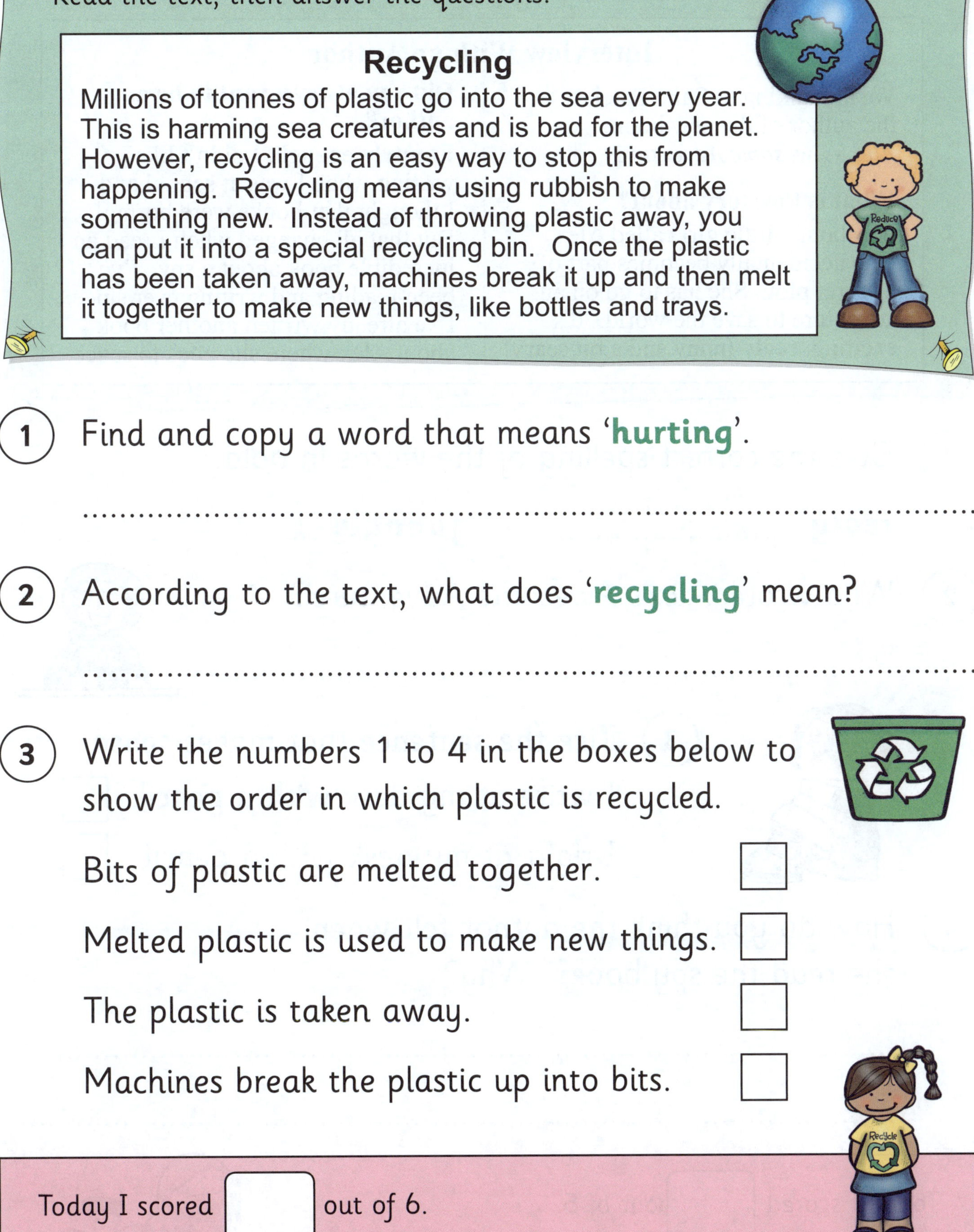

Read the text, then answer the questions.

Recycling

Millions of tonnes of plastic go into the sea every year. This is harming sea creatures and is bad for the planet. However, recycling is an easy way to stop this from happening. Recycling means using rubbish to make something new. Instead of throwing plastic away, you can put it into a special recycling bin. Once the plastic has been taken away, machines break it up and then melt it together to make new things, like bottles and trays.

1 Find and copy a word that means '**hurting**'.

....

2 According to the text, what does '**recycling**' mean?

....

3 Write the numbers 1 to 4 in the boxes below to show the order in which plastic is recycled.

Bits of plastic are melted together. ☐

Melted plastic is used to make new things. ☐

The plastic is taken away. ☐

Machines break the plastic up into bits. ☐

Today I scored ☐ out of 6.

Week 6 — Day 5

Read the text, then answer the questions.

Interview With an Author

We are talking to Saira Patel, the author of the new book *Alex's Awesome Adventure*.

What is the story about?
It's about a little girl called Alex who accidentally becomes part of a secret plot. She has to go on an adventure to save the world. It's exciting, **realy** funny and a bit scary!

Did you always want to be an author?
Funnyly enough, I didn't like writing when I was at school and I thought that books were boring! But that all changed when I read an incredible book about a spy. I've been reading and writing ever since. I've already written another book about Alex where she goes to space.

1. Give the correct spelling of the words in bold.

   realy ....   **funnyly** ....

2. Who wrote 'Alex's Awesome Adventure'?

   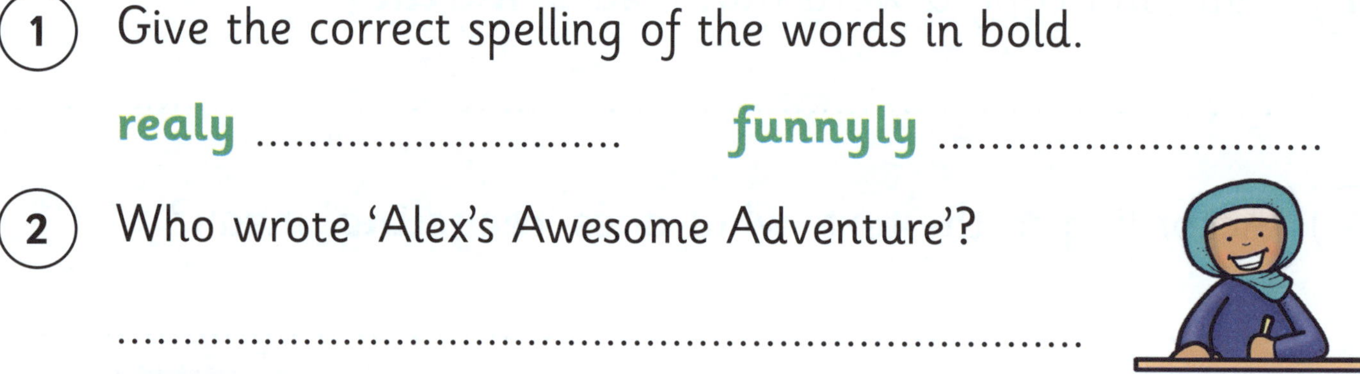

   ....

3. Tick the sentence that makes sense.

   I write at my desk with a pencil. ☐

   I right at my desk with a pencil. ☐

4. How do you think the author felt when she read the spy book? Why?

   ....

   ....

Today I scored ☐ out of 5.

Week 7 — Day 1

Read each sentence, then circle the correct spelling of the word in bold.

I am **great** / **grait** at archery.

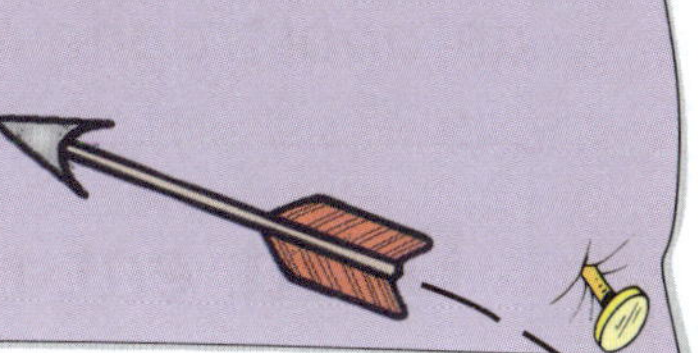

1. My archery **clas** / **class** was fun.

2. **Mistar** / **Mr** Jago taught us how to aim.

3. We learnt how to **holed** / **hold** the bow.

4. Kian wants to **improove** / **improve** his archery.

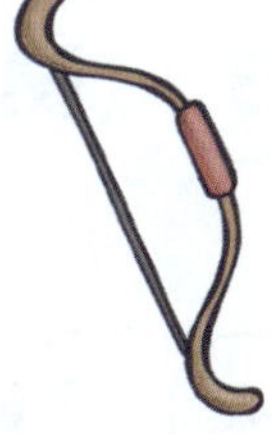

5. **Moest** / **Most** of the arrows missed.

6. **Who** / **Hoo** fired that arrow?

7. I wish that I **could** / **cud** hit the target.

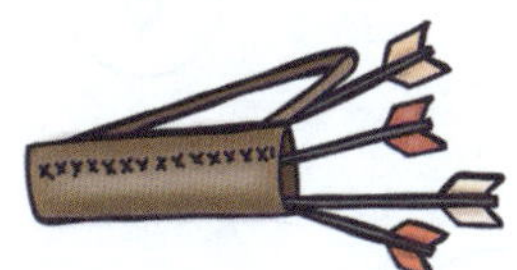

8. The **children** / **childs** love doing archery.

9. Polly **ownly** / **only** has three arrows left.

Today I scored [ ] out of 9.

Year 2 English — Summer Term

Week 7 — Day 2

Rewrite each word in bold using an apostrophe in the correct place.

Dont eat the doughnut! .... Don't ....

1 **Were** going to the doughnut shop. ....

2 **Amys** mum had a jam doughnut. ....

3 **Maliks** treat has caramel icing. ....

4 **Theyve** got a great selection! ....

5 **Im** not hungry. ....

6 **Lilas** saving half for later. ....

7 **Youve** got icing on your face. ....

8 **Tonys** choice was a good one. ....

Today I scored [   ] out of 8.

Week 7 — Day 3

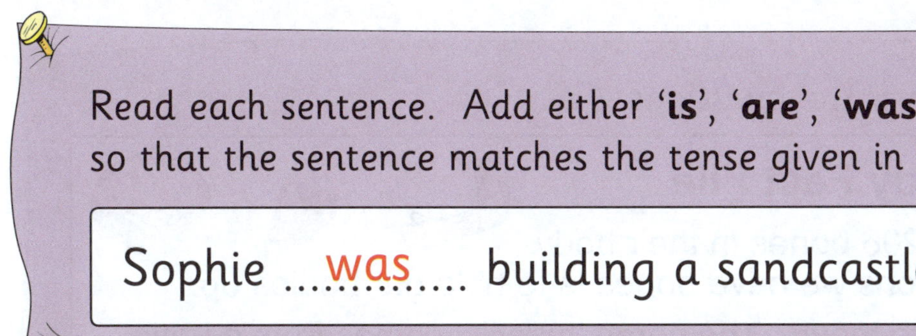

Read each sentence. Add either '**is**', '**are**', '**was**' or '**were**' so that the sentence matches the tense given in brackets.

Sophie .....**was**..... building a sandcastle. (**past**)

(1) Craig .... digging a hole. (**past**)

(2) They .... throwing a ball. (**present**)

(3) James .... wearing sunglasses. (**past**)

(4) Andy .... reading a book. (**present**)

(5) They .... eating ice lollies. (**past**)

(6) Sandy .... drinking a smoothie. (**past**)

(7) Sonia .... taking a photo. (**present**)

(8) They .... sitting in the sun. (**present**)

Today I scored ☐ out of 8.

Year 2 English — Summer Term

Week 7 — Day 4

Read the text, then answer the questions.

The Human Body Fact File

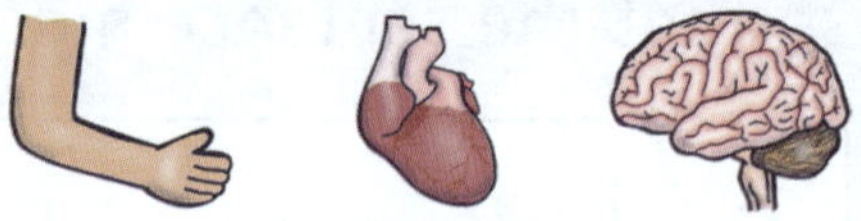

- An adult human has 206 bones in their body.
  One of the main reasons we have bones is to hold our bodies up.
- Our muscles help us to move. The name 'muscle' comes from a Latin word meaning 'little mouse'. This is because muscles moving under the skin reminded people of mice moving under a rug or carpet.
- The heart pumps blood around the body. An adult heart is usually around the size of a fist and beats over 100 000 times every day.
- The brain tells the body what to do. The brain is so important that it uses almost a quarter of the body's energy, even though it's quite small.

(1) How many bones are there in an adult human body?

....

(2) What does '**muscle**' mean in Latin?

....

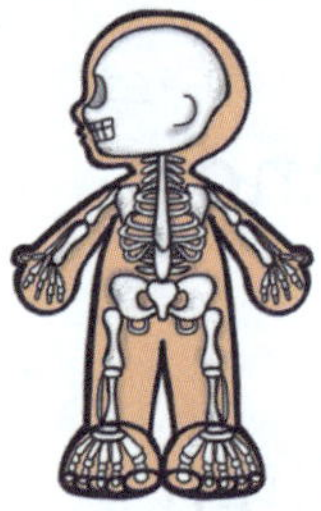

(3) What is the size of an adult heart compared to in the text?

....

(4) Write 'true' or 'false' for each sentence.

Bones help to support our bodies. ....

The heart pumps water around the body. ....

The body is controlled by the brain. ....

Today I scored ☐ out of 6.

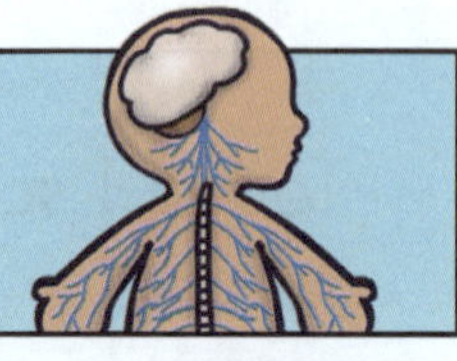

Week 7 — Day 5

Read the text, then answer the questions.

The Discovery

When Pippa was growing up, her **pearents** were often busy with work. Every weekend, Pippa helped them with the chores. One day, when Pippa was emptying the bin, she heard a strange voice. It seemed to be coming from inside the bin. At first, she thought she was imagining it, but then she heard it again.

"Help me!" the voice squeaked. Pippa looked **beehind** her, but no one was there. She peered into the bin and let out a gasp. The eyes of a slimy, green bin monster stared back at her.

(1) Give the correct spelling of the words in bold.

pearents .... **beehind** ....

(2) What tense is the phrase '**Pippa was growing up**' in?

present ☐ past ☐

(3) Why do you think Pippa '**let out a gasp**'?

....

....

(4) Rewrite the phrase below using an apostrophe.

Pippas discovery ....

Today I scored ☐ out of 5.

          Year 2 English — Summer Term

Week 8 — Day 1

The Easter Bunny has started collecting eggs for next Easter, but only those with correctly spelt words are made of chocolate. Help him by circling the chocolate eggs and crossing the words with incorrect spellings. Then, write down how many chocolate eggs there are.

1. treasure

2. hopping

3. donky

4. familys

5. emoshun

6. wrapper

7. hideing

8. celebrate

9. table

10. luvely

11. How many chocolate eggs are there?

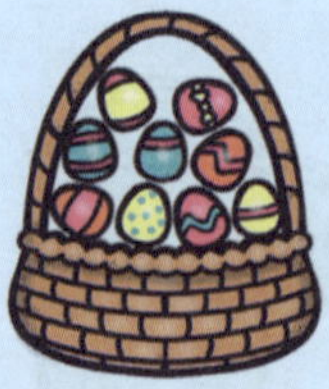

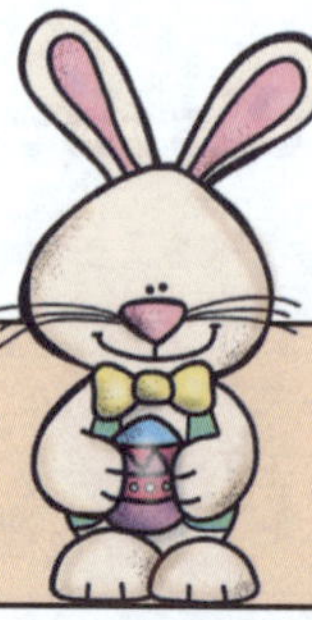

Today I scored [ ] out of 11.

Week 8 — Day 2

Underline the mistake in each of the sentences below.

We <u>is</u> both watching a drama.

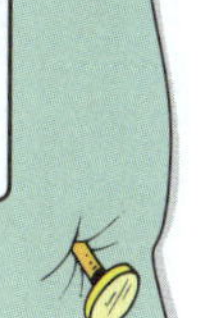

1 They was watching the new episode together.

2 She watches the show after school yesterday.

3 Shall we watch a comedy but a drama?

4 Last year, I bought a house because I win the game show.

5 Vani laughed loud at the television.

6 He are watching the news by himself.

7 This series is funniest than the last.

8 Bilal didn't turn the TV off until he is forgetful.

9 That I get home, I watch television.

Today I scored [ ] out of 9.

   Year 2 English — Summer Term

Week 8 — Day 3

Use the words from the boxes to complete the
sentences below. You should only use each word once.

| and |

We cooked burgers ....**and**............ sausages.

| are | | was | | when | | that |

| made | | longest | | hotter |

1) We .... the salad yesterday.

2) Dad .... grilling some vegetable skewers.

3) It is .... today than it was last week.

4) My brothers .... serving drinks.

5) Tell me .... the veggie burger is done.

6) This is the steak .... I want to eat.

7) The chicken takes the .... to cook.

Today I scored [   ] out of 7.

Week 8 — Day 4

Read the text, then answer the questions.

Easy Homemade Ice Cream

Step 1: Whisk 600 ml of double cream for around three minutes.

Step 2: Slowly add 400 ml of sweetened condensed milk.

Step 3: Add a teaspoon of vanilla extract (this will stop the ice cream getting too hard in the freezer).

Step 4: Mix in your choice of flavourings. You could try crushed biscuits, chunks of fruit or chocolate chips.

Step 5: Pour the mixture into a container and place it in the freezer to set for at least three hours before eating.

1) According to the text, what should you do first?

Whisk the cream. ☐   Mix in your flavourings. ☐

2) Which word in the text means the same as 'firm'?

sweetened ☐   hard ☐   crushed ☐

3) What do you think would happen to the ice cream if you forgot to add the vanilla extract?

....

4) Why do you need to leave the mixture in the freezer for at least three hours before eating?

....

Today I scored ☐ out of 4.

          Year 2 English — Summer Term

Week 8 — Day 5

Read the poem, then answer the questions.

Bertha Bear

When winter rears its **icey** head,
Bertha Bear goes back to bed.
The frosty winds may howl and rave,
But Bertha stays inside her cave.
She naps all day and yawns all night,
Till the winter **munths** are out of sight.
Then as spring flowers start to grow,
Bertha comes out and says, "Hello!"

1) Write the correct spelling of the words in bold.

icey ....   **munths** ....

2) Where does Bertha live?

....

3) What does Bertha do during the days in winter?

....

4) Circle the correct word to complete this sentence.

Bertha only comes out **that / when** winter is over.

Today I scored ☐ out of 5.

Week 9 — Day 1

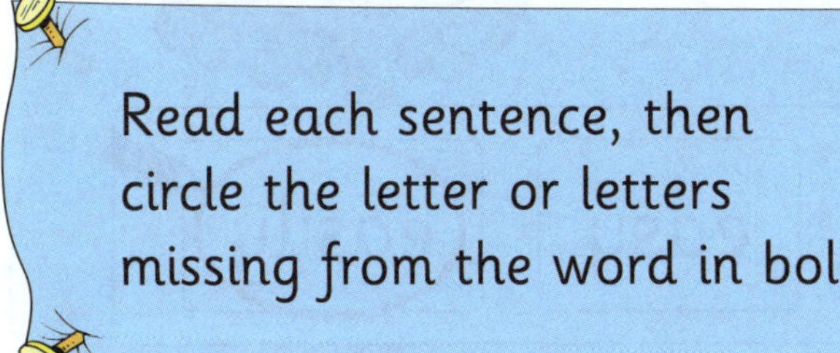

Read each sentence, then circle the letter or letters missing from the word in bold.

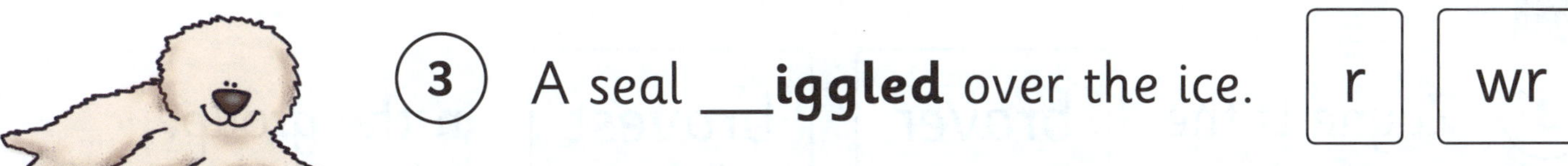

1 The dogs pulled the explorer's **sle__**.

ge | dge

2 He couldn't **s__** very far in the snowstorm.

ea | ee

3 A seal **__iggled** over the ice.

r | wr

4 The Arctic Ocean is mostly covered by **i__**.

se | ce

5 The snowmobile moved **quick__**.

ly | ily

6 Asif saw **sever__** polar bears.

al | el

7 The walrus was **rela__ing** in the sun.

x | xx

8 The puffin **fl__** across the sky.

ies | ys

Today I scored [ ] out of 8.

Year 2 English — Summer Term

Week 9 — Day 2

Circle the correct word to complete each sentence.

I reached the top **easy** **easily** .

1) Yesterday I **climbed** **climbing** a tree.

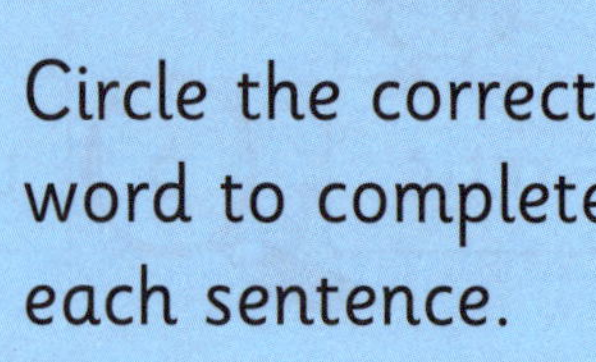

2) The branches are rough **and** **but** spiky.

3) Zayne is the **braver** **bravest** in the group.

4) Grant chose to climb the tree **slowly** **slowlly** .

5) I started climbing the tree **if** **that** had red leaves.

6) Ahmed was **walking** **walked** on the branch.

7) Be **careless** **careful** on that thin branch!

8) Jenny nearly **fell** **fall** from the tree.

Today I scored ☐ out of 8.

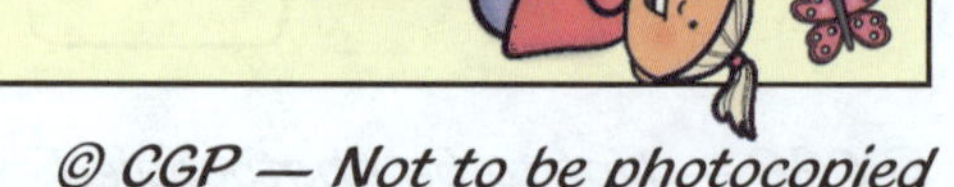

Week 9 — Day 3

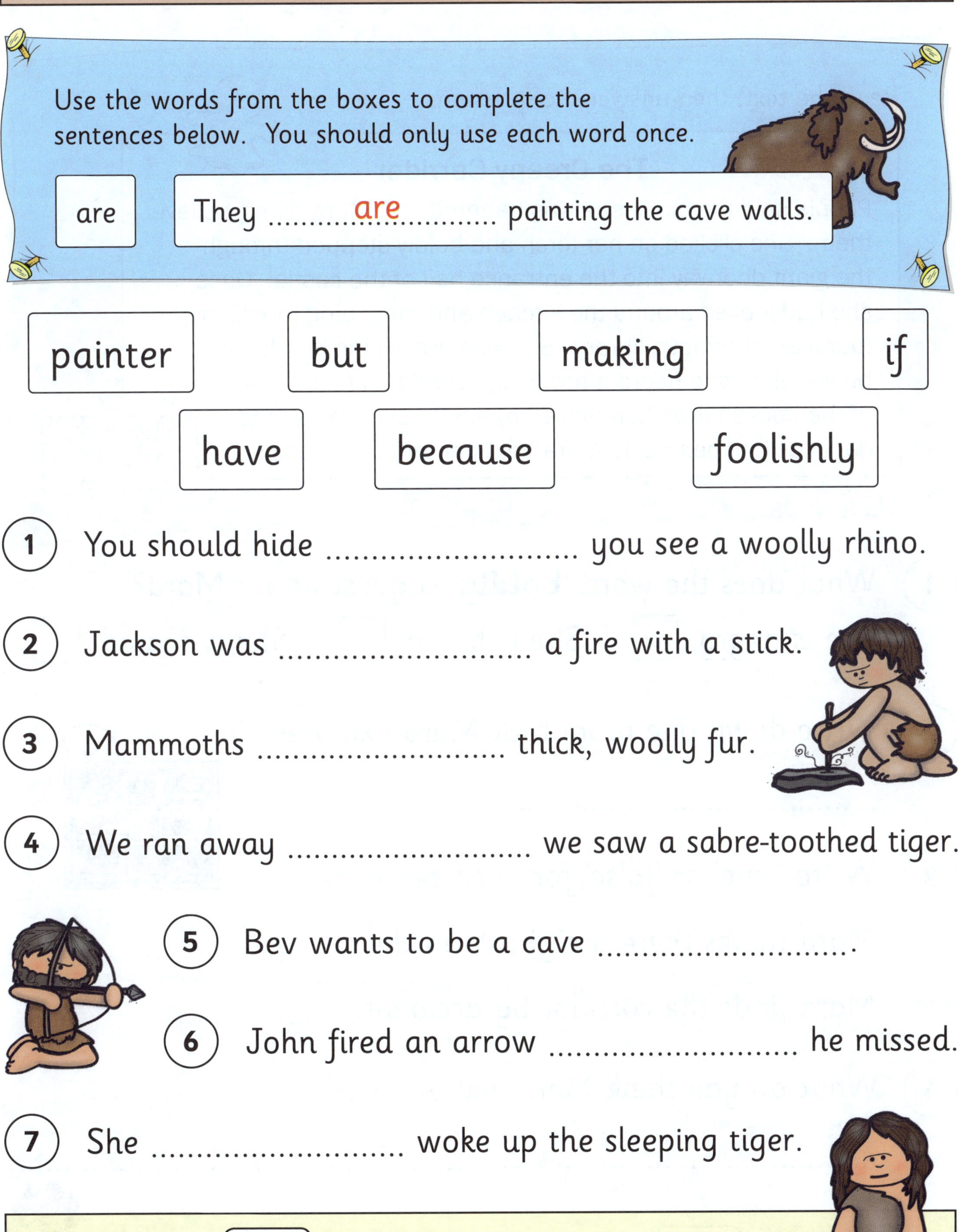

Use the words from the boxes to complete the sentences below. You should only use each word once.

| are | They .... are .... painting the cave walls. |

painter | but | making | if

have | because | foolishly

1. You should hide .... you see a woolly rhino.

2. Jackson was .... a fire with a stick.

3. Mammoths .... thick, woolly fur.

4. We ran away .... we saw a sabre-toothed tiger.

5. Bev wants to be a cave ....

6. John fired an arrow .... he missed.

7. She .... woke up the sleeping tiger.

Today I scored [ ] out of 7.

   Year 2 English — Summer Term

Week 9 — Day 4

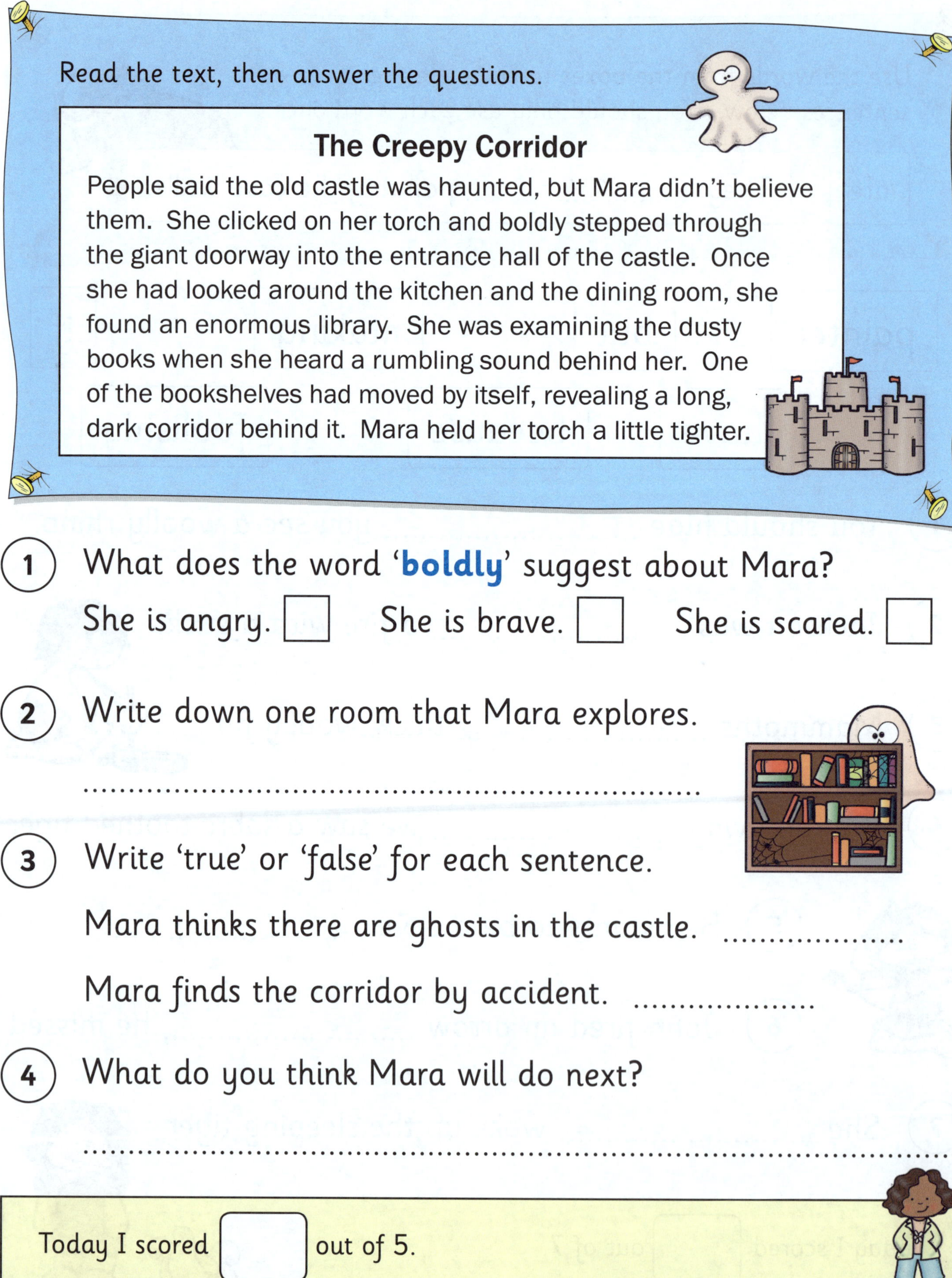

Read the text, then answer the questions.

The Creepy Corridor

People said the old castle was haunted, but Mara didn't believe them. She clicked on her torch and boldly stepped through the giant doorway into the entrance hall of the castle. Once she had looked around the kitchen and the dining room, she found an enormous library. She was examining the dusty books when she heard a rumbling sound behind her. One of the bookshelves had moved by itself, revealing a long, dark corridor behind it. Mara held her torch a little tighter.

1) What does the word '**boldly**' suggest about Mara?

She is angry. ☐   She is brave. ☐   She is scared. ☐

2) Write down one room that Mara explores.

....

3) Write 'true' or 'false' for each sentence.

Mara thinks there are ghosts in the castle. ....

Mara finds the corridor by accident. ....

4) What do you think Mara will do next?

....

Today I scored ☐ out of 5.

Week 9 — Day 5

Read the text, then answer the questions.

Chinese New Year

It was starting to get dark, but the **hole** street was glowing with red lanterns. Chinese New Year was Ping's favourite day and the parade was about to start. The drumming began. It started slowly at first, but got faster and faster. Ping thought that it sounded like a heartbeat speeding up in excitement. Suddenly, a majestic dragon started **weaveing** through the streets. Ping couldn't take his eyes off it. Although it was mostly made out of fabric, it seemed to have a life of its own.

1 Write the correct spelling of the words in bold.

hole ....   **weaveing** ....

2 What type of sentence is '**The drumming began.**'?

command ☐   exclamation ☐   statement ☐

3 Find and copy an adjective that is used to describe the Chinese dragon.

....

4 How do you think Ping felt while watching the parade? Explain your answer.

....

....

Today I scored ☐ out of 5.

    Year 2 English — Summer Term

Week 10 — Day 1

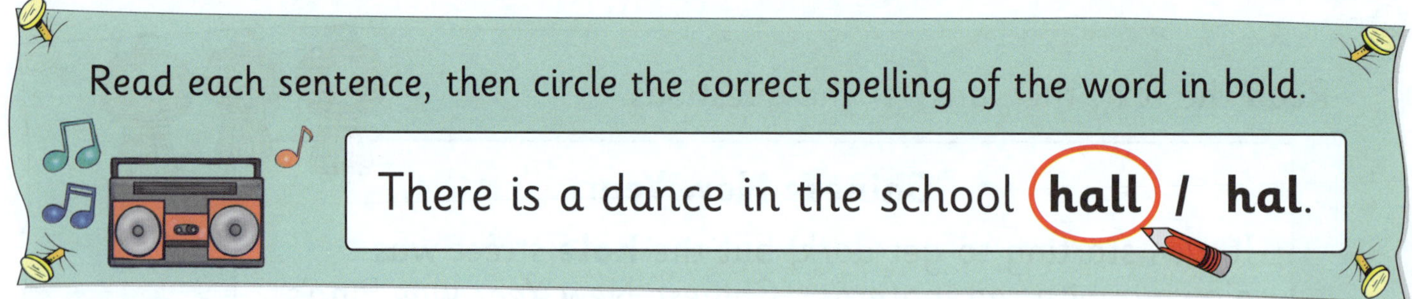

Read each sentence, then circle the correct spelling of the word in bold.

There is a dance in the school **hall** / **hal**.

1. The dance takes place on **Monday** / **Munday**.

2. Jen danced in the **middle** / **middal** of the room.

3. Kevin taps his foot on the **flor** / **floor**.

4. Her shoes are very **shiny** / **shiney**.

5. He **trys** / **tries** to copy our dance moves.

6. Cho bends her **nees** / **knees** in time to the beat.

7. Kofi wants **too** / **to** be the best dancer.

8. My favourite hobby is **dancing** / **danceing**.

9. They twirl **beautifully** / **beautyfully**.

Today I scored ☐ out of 9.

Week 10 — Day 2

The words in bold below are spelt incorrectly.
Write the correct spellings on the lines.

Jan **nows** how to make scones. ....knows............

(1) I **bakeed** brownies. ....

(2) We **wotched** the cakes rise. ....

(3) Biscuits contain lots of **shugar**. ....

(4) My mum made an **appil** cake. ....

(5) Jamal put the cookies in the **uven**. ....

(6) It is **allmost** ready. ....

(7) We **fri** the pancakes. ....

(8) The fresh bread is still **waum**. ....

Today I scored [ ] out of 8.

Year 2 English — Summer Term

Week 10 — Day 3

Circle the punctuation error in each of these sentences.

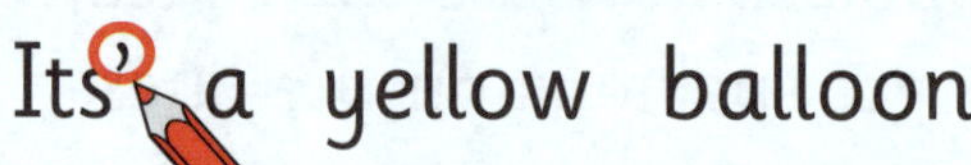

1. Karen cant blow up her balloon.

2. A party needs cake. friends and balloons.

3. She didnt' hold onto the string.

4. Why are you floating in the air.

5. Astrid blew up her' balloon.

6. What fun making balloon animals is.

7. We are definitely playing with balloons?

8. Joe, Lesley and Karim, are kicking the balloons.

9. how did you make a dog out of balloons?

Today I scored [ ] out of 9.

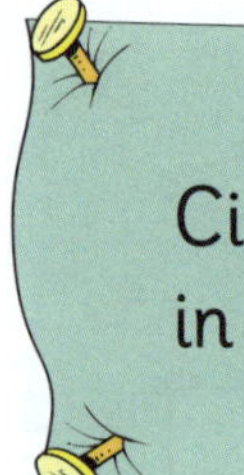
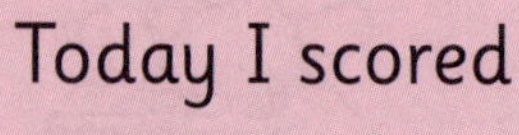

Week 10 — Day 4

Read the text, then answer the questions.

The Magic Show

The show began with smoke clouds and flashing lights. Mike stepped out onto the stage and smiled widely. Tonight was the night. He was finally performing his first show as a proper magician.

"Welcome everyone!" he shouted. His voice echoed around the large theatre. "Prepare to be amazed!"

Suddenly, the room was plunged into darkness. A few seconds later, the lights turned back on. The audience let out a huge gasp. Mike had disappeared.

1 Give two special effects Mike uses at the start of his show.

.... and ....

2 Which word is the closest in meaning to '**proper**'?

real ☐   new ☐   exciting ☐   poor ☐

3 Write 'true' or 'false' for each sentence.

Mike looks happy on the stage. ....

The lights stayed off for a long time. ....

4 How do you think the audience feels when the lights come back on? Explain your answer.

....

....

Today I scored ☐ out of 6.

Week 10 — Day 5

Read the text, then answer the questions.

St Bernard Rescue Dogs

St Bernards are a very large and strong type of dog. They are also known for being excellent mountain search and rescue dogs. For hundreds of years, St Bernards have been used to rescue people from the Alps, a range of mountains in Europe. The Alps can be difficult mountains to **clim**, especially in snowy weather. St Bernards are brilliant rescue dogs **becos** of their amazing sense of smell. It helps them to find and save the lives of people who have become buried in the snow.

1 Write the correct spelling of the words in bold.

clim .... **becos** ....

2 What kind of weather makes the Alps even more difficult?

....

3 How are St Bernards able to find people buried in the snow?

....

4 Tick the sentence that uses commas correctly.

They are large, strong and gentle dogs. ☐

They are large, strong and, gentle dogs. ☐

Today I scored ☐ out of 5.

Week 11 — Day 1

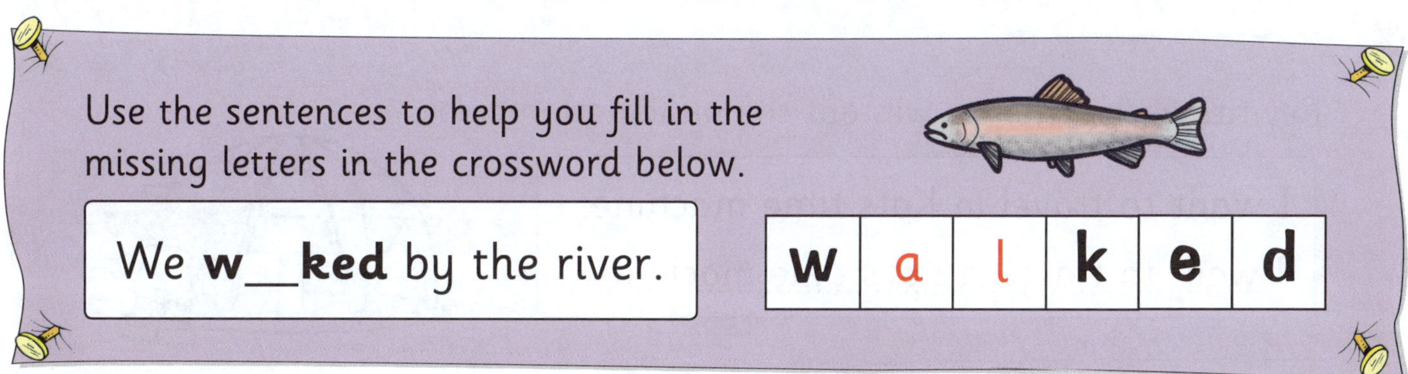

Use the sentences to help you fill in the missing letters in the crossword below.

We **w__ked** by the river.

w	a	l	k	e	d

(1) There are lots of **li_t__** fish. 

(2) The **weas__** came to the river for a drink.

(3) There is a **bri__e** we can use to cross the water.

(4) We swim when the weather is **w__m**.

(5) The otters float along **h_pp___**.

(6) The frogs eat lots of **f__es**.

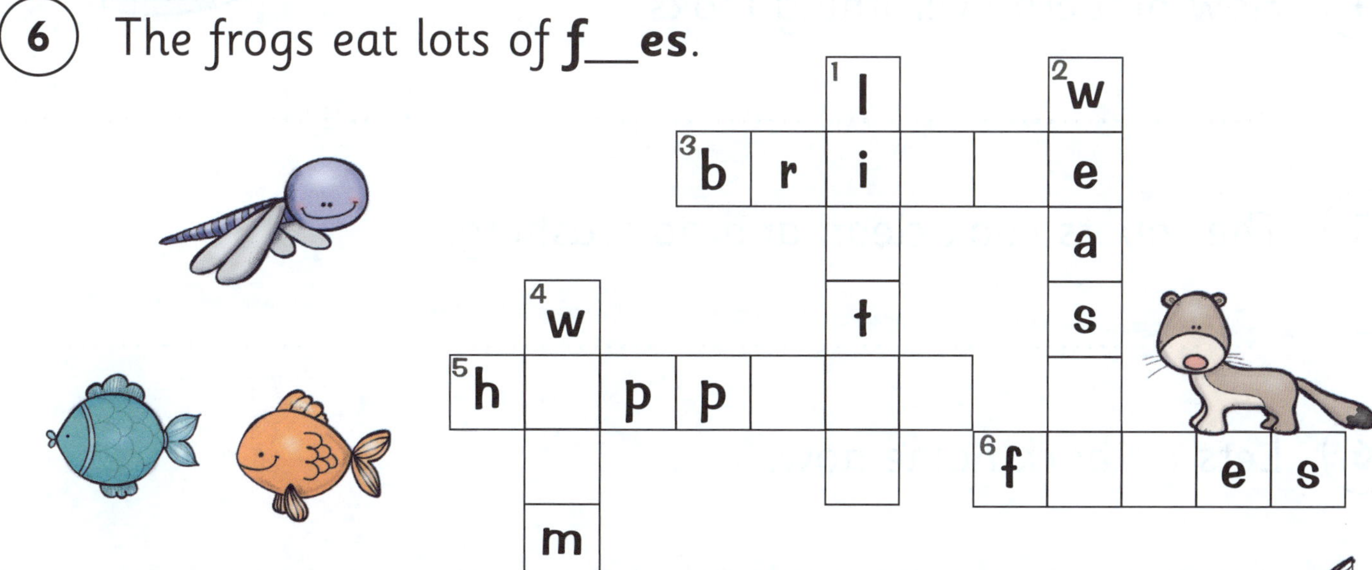

Today I scored [ ] out of 6.

Week 11 — Day 2

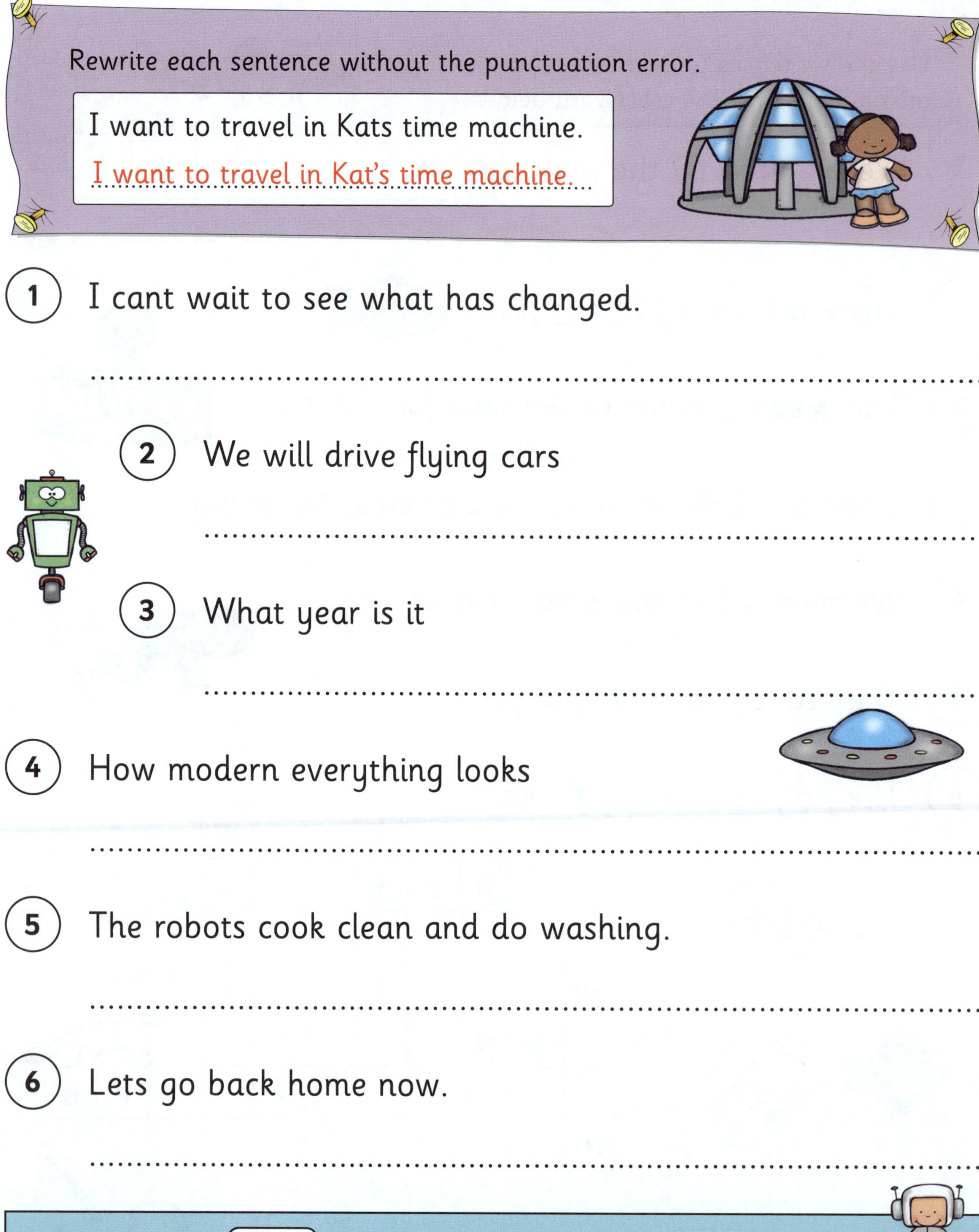

Rewrite each sentence without the punctuation error.

I want to travel in Kats time machine.
I want to travel in Kat's time machine.

1 I cant wait to see what has changed.

....

2 We will drive flying cars

....

3 What year is it

....

4 How modern everything looks

....

5 The robots cook clean and do washing.

....

6 Lets go back home now.

....

Today I scored [   ] out of 6.

Week 11 — Day 3

The words in bold below are spelt incorrectly.
Write the correct spellings on the lines.

My hair isn't **drie**. ....dry..............

1. Matt put **jel** in his hair. ....

2. Elena **tryed** to put lipstick on. ....

3. My hair is so **shinie**. ....

4. Preya is **cuting** my hair. ....

5. My sister **riggles** when I do her nails. ....

6. This **losion** smells really good. ....

7. My **bruther** never brushes his hair. ....

8. Freya puts cream on her **fase**. ....

9. The salon is **uzually** busy. ....

Today I scored [ ] out of 9.

   Year 2 English — Summer Term

Week 11 — Day 4

Read the text, then answer the questions.

The Parthenon

The Parthenon is one of the most famous buildings in Greece. It was built by the Ancient Greeks nearly 2500 years ago and took 15 years to complete. It has survived many disasters over the years, including fires, earthquakes, wars and even an explosion in 1687. The Parthenon is part of a group of temples that were built on a hill in the city of Athens. Together, they are known as the Acropolis, which is Greek for "high city".

1) How long did it take to build the Parthenon?

2500 years ☐   15 years ☐   1687 years ☐

2) Give two disasters that the Parthenon has survived.

.... and ....

3) Write 'true' or 'false' for each sentence.

No one has heard of the Parthenon. ....

The Acropolis is in Athens. ....

4) What does 'Acropolis' mean?

....

Today I scored ☐ out of 6.

Week 11 — Day 5

Read the text, then answer the questions.

Daisy the Lazy Cow

Of all the cows in all the fields, Daisy was the **lazyest**. While the other cows liked to run around the field and play in the mud, Daisy was happy sitting in her corner and munching on the grass.

One sunny morning, Daisy was taking her third nap of the day when her friend Caspar came over and woke her up.

"Hurry," he said excitedly, "the farmer has left the kitchen door open and we are helping ourselves to as much food as we like!"

Daisy stood up straight away. There was one thing she liked more than **naping**, and that was food.

1 Write the correct spelling of the words in bold.

lazyest .... **naping** ....

2 Give one activity that the other cows enjoy doing.

....

3 Add one punctuation mark to the sentence below.

Daisy likes sleeping eating and relaxing.

4 What do you think will happen next in the story?

....

....

Today I scored [ ] out of 5.

Year 2 English — Summer Term

Week 12 — Day 1

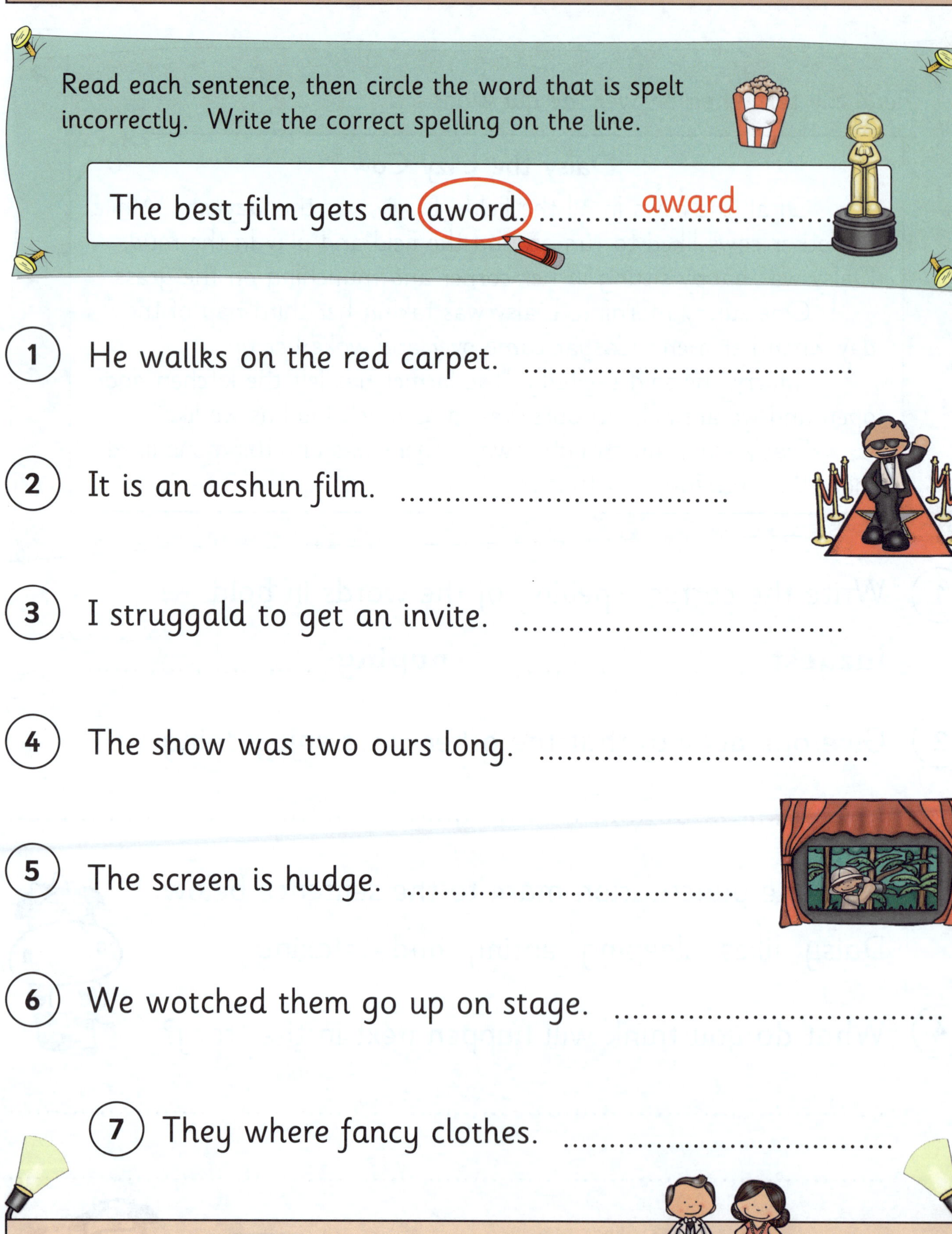

Read each sentence, then circle the word that is spelt incorrectly. Write the correct spelling on the line.

The best film gets an (aword.) .... award ....

1) He wallks on the red carpet. ....

2) It is an acshun film. ....

3) I struggald to get an invite. ....

4) The show was two ours long. ....

5) The screen is hudge. ....

6) We wotched them go up on stage. ....

7) They where fancy clothes. ....

Today I scored ☐ out of 14.

Week 12 — Day 2

Underline the mistake in each of the sentences below.

1) Yesterday, I went to the shop and buys lemons. 

2) You can add ice but sugar to your drink.

3) Talia's cup is fullest than Max's cup. 

4) All the lemons was so sour and juicy.

5) Ivy was carful to not spill her drink. 

6) Jari were enjoying his fresh lemonade.

7) They drank their lemonade greedyly. 

8) I am squeezes the lemons as fast as I can.

9) I will find more lemons that I run out. 

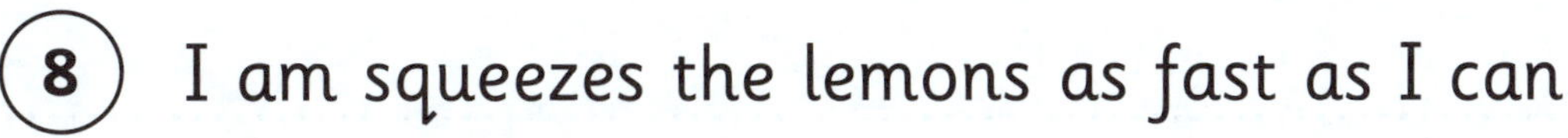

Today I scored [ ] out of 9.

Week 12 — Day 3

Each sentence below has three punctuation errors. Rewrite them without these errors.

we ate at the diner on tuesday

We ate at the diner on Tuesday.

1 Jack Liam and i havent got our milkshakes yet.

....

....

2 Ellies skates are softer shinier and comfier than ben's.

....

....

3 why wont the machine play the song

....

....

Today I scored ☐ out of 9.

Week 12 — Day 4

Read the text, then answer the questions.

The Headache

Lia was having a bad day. She had woken up with a headache and it hadn't gone away. In music class, people played the drums and it got worse. Then, when she got home, her dad was drilling holes in the wall. No matter how hard Lia pressed her hands over her ears, it was no use.

Then she decided to try something else. She lay down on the sofa, closed her eyes and thought about a quieter place. A place where birds chirped in trees and leaves rustled softly in the breeze. She took a deep breath and finally felt the pain in her head start to go away.

1) Write down one noise that was bothering Lia.

....

2) Why do you think Lia puts her hands over her ears?

....

3) What place does Lia imagine going to? Tick one box.

a desert ☐   a forest ☐   a lake ☐

4) How do you think Lia feels at the end of the text? Why?

....

....

Today I scored [ ] out of 4.

Week 12 — Day 5

Read the text, then answer the questions.

Sea Turtles

Although sea turtles spend most of their lives in the ocean, they are born on beaches. When a female sea turtle is ready to lay her eggs, she crawls onto the sand and digs a hole with her flippers. She stores her eggs inside the hole and covers it with sand to keep the eggs safe from other **animels**. When the baby turtles are ready to hatch, they break open their shells and **riggle** out onto the beach. They scurry into the ocean as quickly as they can and disappear beneath the sparkling blue waves.

1 Give the correct spelling of the words in bold.

animels .... **riggle** ....

2 How does the female turtle keep her eggs safe?

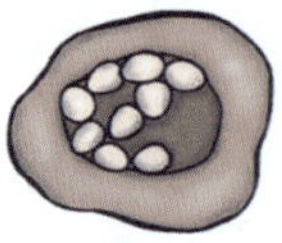

....

....

3 Tick the sentence that stays in the same tense.

The turtle climbed out of its shell and ran to the sea. ☐

The turtle climbed out of its shell and runs to the sea. ☐

4 Write down one adjective used to describe the waves.

....

Today I scored ☐ out of 5.

Answers

Week 1 — Day 1

1. The **treasure** was in the pyramid.
2. The **other** mummy was much scarier.
3. I waved my hand to **swat** away the fly.
4. A **swarm** of insects ate the crops.
5. We set off on the long **journey**.
6. The queen **walked** by the river.
7. They **worked** hard on the statue.
8. I couldn't see in the **darkness** of the tomb.
9. I was full of **excitement** to visit Egypt.

Week 1 — Day 2

1. powerful
2. harmless
3. grateful
4. forgetful
5. useless
6. thoughtless
7. spotless
8. beautiful

Week 1 — Day 3

1. Nan promised us some crumbs **if** we behaved.
2. Mia hid in the nest **because** she was scared.
3. We ran away **when** the humans were near.
4. Leo's whiskers twitch **when** he's confused.
5. His ears pricked up **if** he was angry.
6. I like any dish **that** has cheese in it.
7. Em had grey fur **that** was just like her dad's.
8. Lou gave a squeak **because** she was excited.

Week 1 — Day 4

1. three
2. perfect
3. fill in a (simple) form
4. a chocolate fountain party / a baking competition

Week 1 — Day 5

1. bright
2. Pia was lying down **when** she saw a shooting star.
3. gold
4. Pia thought the stars were wonder**ful**.

Week 2 — Day 1

1. yes
2. yes
3. no
4. yes
5. no
6. no
7. yes
8. no

Week 2 — Day 2

1. Ruby
2. Liz
3. Abe
4. Ben
5. **Liz** and **Ben**
   (1 mark for each)

Week 2 — Day 3

1. Kina needs to pack **shorts, boots and jeans.**
2. Jason needs to pack **a hat, a scarf and a coat.**
3. Lewis needs to pack **a vest, a shirt and a jacket.**
4. Tess needs to pack **boots, a jumper and a skirt.**

Week 2 — Day 4

1. to move from side to side
2. by the lake
3. The elves get dressed up for the party. — true
   The party finishes in the afternoon. — false
   (1 mark for each)
4. No. The poem says the party only happens once a year.

Week 2 — Day 5

1. balls, usually
   (1 mark for each)
2. command
3. Ingredients include butter, sugar and eggs.
4. Any two from:
   a wooden spoon / a large bowl / a tray / an oven
   (1 mark for each)

Week 3 — Day 1

1. hockey
2. world
3. television
4. decision
5. brother
6. warm
7. awarded
8. amazement

Week 3 — Day 2

1. "Can you shuffle the cards, Beth**?**" I asked. Beth gave me ten cards. "**D**on't look at what cards I have!" I shouted.
2. Let's make a tower. **W**hat colour blocks should we use**?** How beautiful it looks!
3. "What a great game chess is!" Cam said excitedly. "**W**e play it every Sunday. Do you want to go first**?**"
4. **S**hall we play hide and seek**?** I'll count to twenty. Hooray, I've found you!

(For each question, there is 1 mark for each punctuation mark and 1 mark for the capital letter.)

Week 3 — Day 3

1. Ashley is **making** the pizza dough.
2. She is **rolling** it out carefully.
3. Marco **is** tossing it in the air.
4. I **am** mixing the tomato sauce.
5. Jane is **spreading** the sauce.
6. We **are** adding the toppings.
7. He is **putting** it in the oven.
8. I am **slicing** the pizza equally.
9. They **are** eating the pizza.

Week 3 — Day 4

1. The café is the first place Robin stole from. — false
   Robin was found in a cupboard. — true
   (1 mark for each)
2. a large cheesecake
3. owned up
4. Robin ate it.

Week 3 — Day 5

1. pleasure, water
   (1 mark for each)
2. Sam **is sitting** in the little boat.
3. E.g. so that he can fish again
4. He becomes more excited about it.

Week 4 — Day 1

1. Anya's skateboard
2. Mark's teddy
3. Samira's train
4. Hugh's toy soldier
5. Martha's doll
6. Noah's drum
7. Hannah's car
8. Peter's duck

Week 4 — Day 2

1. Oscar was fear**ful** that a spider would crawl on him.
2. Molly quiet**ly** told her sister a secret.
3. My dog has a loud bark but she's harm**less**.
4. Tim proud**ly** accepted his medal when he won.
5. Jaxon was very forget**ful**.
6. Kameela's necklace was price**less** to her.

| 5 | 6 | 3 | 1 | 2 |

Week 4 — Day 3

1. Sean drives really **quickly**.
2. The truck is painted **weirdly**.
3. My truck **suddenly** stopped working.
4. Amir drives **carelessly**.
5. Angela watched the race **eagerly**.
6. Eli **nervously** waited for the result.
7. Ling **nearly** won the race.

Week 4 — Day 4

1. **invisibility** and **laser fingers** (1 mark for each)
2. sneak
3. Ama wears a superhero mask.
4. E.g. She's saved the world many times before. / She has superpowers.

Week 4 — Day 5

1. hopeless, tuneful (1 mark for each)
2. brightly
3. Dad's / brother's
4. birdsong

Week 5 — Day 1

1. Of all the birds, Flo has the **longest** legs.
2. My beak is **sharper** than yours.
3. The budgie is **quieter** than usual.
4. Pippin is the **proudest** bird of us all.
5. The toucan is **bigger** than me.
6. Hummingbirds are **smaller** than parrots.
7. The **greatest** bird in the group is the puffin.
8. Penguins are **friendlier** than ostriches.
9. The pelican has the **oddest** beak of all birds.

Week 5 — Day 2

1. We ran to the sta**tion**.
2. There was confu**sion** on the platform.
3. Show cau**tion** near the tracks.
4. The train is in mo**tion**.
5. There is a new ver**sion** of my toy train.
6. Which direc**tion** is the train going in?
7. It was my deci**sion** to take the train.
8. We asked at the informa**tion** desk.

Week 5 — Day 3

1. They **were** queuing for the water slide.
2. Jim **was** playing in the fountain.
3. We **were** doing underwater handstands.
4. Dad **was** watching us from the side.
5. Chris and Ava **were** floating down the lazy river.
6. I **was** swimming with my friends.
7. We **were** screaming the whole way down the slide.
8. They **were** changing into swimming trunks.

Week 5 — Day 4

1. hill running
2. the Lake District
3. There are hard rocks. / There is long grass. / The weather can be wild.
4. take part

Week 5 — Day 5

1. attention
2. because it is dark in the mine / so that he can see in the dark mine
3. **wet** and **slippery** (1 mark for each)
4. Kai **was** looking for rubies when he saw the bat.

Week 6 — Day 1

1. Only **one** of them could win.
2. He **won** the jousting contest easily.
3. I **blew** the trumpet when she arrived.
4. The enemy snuck in during the **night**.
5. He is the **son** of the king and queen.
6. She was holding a **blue** shield.
7. The **knight** went on a dangerous journey.
8. The **sun** shone on his armour.

Week 6 — Day 2

1. The mud squelched **loudly**.
2. The pig dashed around the farmyard **quickly**.
3. Mud dripped **slowly** from the pig's face.
4. The pig rolled **playfully** in the mud.
5. The pig smiled **widely** at the farmer.
6. The farmer told the pig off for behaving **badly**.

Week 6 — Day 3

1. The orange (**adjective**) starfish stuck to the tank (**noun**). (1 mark for each)
2. A colourful fish swam (**verb**) past the plants swiftly (**adverb**). (1 mark for each)
3. The jellyfish has long (**adjective**), light blue tentacles (**noun**). (1 mark for each)
4. Hungrily (**adverb**), the shark flashed (**verb**) its shiny white teeth. (1 mark for each)

Week 6 — Day 4

1. harming
2. using rubbish to make something new
3. Bits of plastic are melted together. — 3
   Melted plastic is used to make new things. — 4
   The plastic is taken away. — 1
   Machines break the plastic up into bits. — 2
   (1 mark for each)

Week 6 — Day 5

1. really, funnily (1 mark for each)
2. Saira Patel
3. I write at my desk with a pencil.
4. E.g. She was surprised because she used to think books were boring.

Week 7 — Day 1

1. My archery **class** was fun.
2. **Mr** Jago taught us how to aim.
3. We learnt how to **hold** the bow.
4. Kian wants to **improve** his archery.
5. **Most** of the arrows missed.
6. **Who** fired that arrow?
7. I wish that I **could** hit the target.
8. The **children** love doing archery.
9. Polly **only** has three arrows left.

Week 7 — Day 2

1. We're
2. Amy's
3. Malik's
4. They've
5. I'm
6. Lila's
7. You've
8. Tony's

Week 7 — Day 3

1. Craig **was** digging a hole.
2. They **are** throwing a ball.
3. James **was** wearing sunglasses.
4. Andy **is** reading a book.
5. They **were** eating ice lollies.
6. Sandy **was** drinking a smoothie.
7. Sonia **is** taking a photo.
8. They **are** sitting in the sun.

Week 7 — Day 4

1. 206
2. little mouse
3. a fist
4. Bones help to support our bodies.
   — true
   The heart pumps water around
   the body. — false
   The body is controlled by the
   brain. — true
   (1 mark for each)

Week 7 — Day 5

1. parents, behind
   (1 mark for each)
2. past
3. E.g. because she was surprised to
   see the bin monster
4. Pippa's discovery

Week 8 — Day 1

1. ~~treasure~~
2. ~~hopping~~
3. donky
4. familys
5. emoshun
6. ~~wrapper~~
7. hideing
8. ~~celebrate~~
9. ~~table~~
10. lovely
11. 5 eggs

Week 8 — Day 2

1. They <u>was</u> watching the new episode
   together.
2. She <u>watches</u> the show after school
   yesterday.
3. Shall we watch a comedy <u>but</u>
   a drama?
4. Last year, I bought a house because
   I <u>win</u> the game show.
5. Vani laughed <u>loud</u> at the television.
6. He <u>are</u> watching the news by himself.
7. This series is <u>funniest</u> than the last.
8. Bilal didn't turn the TV off <u>until</u> he
   is forgetful.
9. <u>That</u> I get home, I watch television.

Week 8 — Day 3

1. We **made** the salad yesterday.
2. Dad **was** grilling some vegetable
   skewers.
3. It is **hotter** today than it was
   last week.
4. My brothers **are** serving drinks.
5. Tell me **when** the veggie burger
   is done.
6. This is the steak **that** I want to eat.
7. The chicken takes the **longest**
   to cook.

Week 8 — Day 4

1. Whisk the cream.
2. hard
3. It would get too hard in the freezer.
4. E.g. so that it has time to set

Week 8 — Day 5

1. icy, months
   (1 mark for each)
2. in a cave
3. naps (sleeps)
4. Bertha only comes out **when** winter
   is over.

Week 9 — Day 1

1. The dogs pulled the explorer's
   sle**dge**.
2. He couldn't s**ee** very far in the
   snowstorm.
3. A seal **wr**iggled over the ice.
4. The Arctic Ocean is mostly covered
   by i**ce**.
5. The snowmobile moved quick**ly**.
6. Asif saw sever**al** polar bears.
7. The walrus was rel**ax**ing in the sun.
8. The puffin f**lies** across the sky.

Week 9 — Day 2

1. Yesterday I **climbed** a tree.
2. The branches are rough **and** spiky.
3. Zayne is the **bravest** in the group.
4. Grant chose to climb the tree **slowly**.
5. I started climbing the tree **that** had
   red leaves.
6. Ahmed was **walking** on the branch.
7. Be **careful** on that thin branch!
8. Jenny nearly **fell** from the tree.

Week 9 — Day 3

1. You should hide **if** you see a woolly
   rhino.
2. Jackson was **making** a fire with
   a stick.
3. Mammoths **have** thick, woolly fur.
4. We ran away **because** we saw
   a sabre-toothed tiger.
5. Bev wants to be a cave **painter**.
6. John fired an arrow **but** he missed.
7. She **foolishly** woke up the sleeping
   tiger.

Week 9 — Day 4

1. She is brave.
2. entrance hall / kitchen /
   dining room / library
3. Mara thinks there are ghosts in
   the castle. — false
   Mara finds the corridor by accident.
   — true
   (1 mark for each)
4. E.g. She will go down the corridor.

Week 9 — Day 5

1. whole, weaving
   (1 mark for each)
2. statement
3. majestic
4. E.g. Ping felt amazed. He couldn't
   take his eyes off the dragon.

Week 10 — Day 1

1. The dance takes place on **Monday**.
2. Jen danced in the **middle** of
   the room.
3. Kevin taps his foot on the **floor**.
4. Her shoes are very **shiny**.
5. He **tries** to copy our dance moves.
6. Cho bends her **knees** in time to
   the beat.
7. Kofi wants **to** be the best dancer.
8. My favourite hobby is **dancing**.
9. They twirl **beautifully**.

Answers

Week 10 — Day 2

1. baked   5. oven
2. watched   6. almost
3. sugar   7. fry
4. apple   8. warm

Week 10 — Day 3

1. Karen (cant) blow up her balloon.
2. A party needs cake◯friends and balloons.
3. She didn◯ hold onto the string.
4. Why are you floating in the air◯
5. Astrid blew up her◯ balloon.
6. What fun making balloon animals is◯
7. We are definitely playing with balloons◯
8. Joe, Lesley and Karim, are kicking the balloons◯
9. ◯how did you make a dog out of balloons?

Week 10 — Day 4

1. **smoke clouds** and **flashing lights** (1 mark for each)
2. real
3. Mike looks happy on stage. — true
   The lights stayed off for a long time. — false
   (1 mark for each)
4. E.g. They are surprised because Mike has disappeared.

Week 10 — Day 5

1. climb, because (1 mark for each)
2. snowy weather
3. They have an amazing sense of smell.
4. They are large, strong and gentle dogs.

Week 11 — Day 1

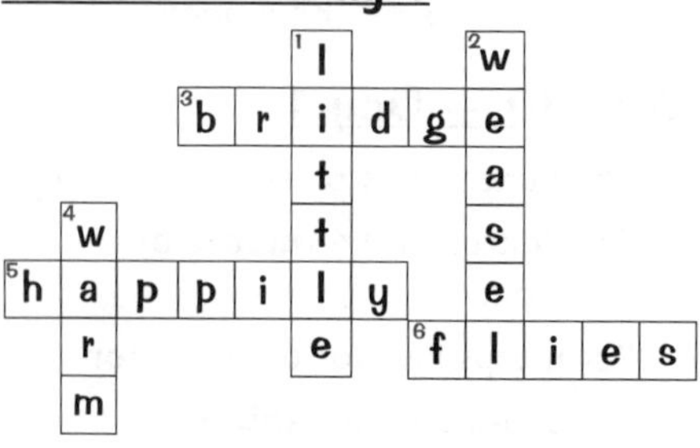

Week 11 — Day 2

1. I can't wait to see what has changed.
2. We will drive flying cars.
3. What year is it**?**
4. How modern everything looks!
5. The robots cook, clean and do washing.
6. Let's go back home now.

Week 11 — Day 3

1. gel   6. lotion
2. tried   7. brother
3. shiny   8. face
4. cutting   9. usually
5. wriggles

Week 11 — Day 4

1. 15 years
2. Any two from:
   fires / earthquakes / wars / an explosion
   (1 mark for each)
3. No one has heard of the Parthenon. — false
   The Acropolis is in Athens. — true
   (1 mark for each)
4. high city

Week 11 — Day 5

1. laziest, napping (1 mark for each)
2. running around the field / playing in the mud
3. Daisy likes sleeping, eating and relaxing.
4. E.g. Daisy will go to the kitchen to eat the food.

Week 12 — Day 1

1. He (wallks) on the red carpet. — walks
2. It is an (acshun) film. — action
3. I (struggald) to get an invite. — struggled
4. The show was two (ours) long. — hours
5. The screen is (hudge) — huge
6. We (wotched) them go up on stage. — watched
7. They (where) fancy clothes. — wear
(For each question, there is 1 mark for each mistake found and 1 mark for each correct spelling.)

Week 12 — Day 2

1. Yesterday, I went to the shop and <u>buys</u> lemons.
2. You can add ice <u>but</u> sugar to your drink.
3. Talia's cup is <u>fullest</u> than Max's cup.
4. All the lemons <u>was</u> so sour and juicy.
5. Ivy was <u>carful</u> to not spill her drink.
6. Jari <u>were</u> enjoying his fresh lemonade.
7. They drank their lemonade <u>greedyly</u>.
8. I am <u>squeezes</u> the lemons as fast as I can.
9. I will find more lemons <u>that</u> I run out.

Week 12 — Day 3

1. Jack, Liam and **I** haven't got our milkshakes yet. (1 mark for each)
2. Ellie's skates are softer, shinier and comfier than **B**en's. (1 mark for each)
3. **W**hy won't the machine play the song**?** (1 mark for each)

Week 12 — Day 4

1. people playing the drums / her dad drilling holes in the wall
2. to block out the noise
3. a forest
4. E.g. She feels relaxed because her headache is going away.

Week 12 — Day 5

1. animals, wriggle (1 mark for each)
2. She stores her eggs in a hole under the sand and covers it up.
3. The turtle climbed out of its shell and ran to the sea.
4. sparkling / blue

E2WSU11